A Study of **Communism**

A Study of **Communism**

J. Edgar Hoover

 Holt, Rinehart and Winston, Inc.
New York · Chicago
San Francisco · Toronto

J. EDGAR HOOVER is eminently qualified as an authority on communism. Since 1924, he has been Director of the Federal Bureau of Investigation, the broad responsibilities of which include jurisdiction in internal security matters involving communism, espionage, sabotage, and related subversive activities. In fulfilling these responsibilities, the FBI conducts numerous investigations and extensive research regarding all phases of Communist activity. *A Study of Communism,* an outgrowth of Mr. Hoover's long, first-hand experience, provides a penetrating analysis of the Communist threat to freedom.

Published simultaneously in Canada by Holt, Rinehart and Winston of Canada, Limited.

Published, October, 1962
Second Printing, September, 1962

Library of Congress Catalog Card Number: 62–20617

83729–0312
Printed in the United States of America

Foreword

Today's headlines remind us there has been no basic change in Communist imperialism. The danger which world communism presents to the free nations has not abated. If anything, it has increased. We will not be able to preserve and develop adequately our heritage of freedom without continually adding to our knowledge of the nature of communism and its totalitarian objectives.

What is communism? What gives communism its dynamic character? What have been the contributions of Marx, Engels, Lenin, Stalin, and Khrushchev to the development of the world Communist movement? How does communism come to power? How has the Communist empire expanded? What are the attractions of communism? Why do people become disillusioned with communism? Why is our free society inherently superior to communism? The answers to these and many other questions are included in this book. It is hoped that this information will not only inform the reader about communism but also develop within him a deeper awareness of the superiority of our heritage of freedom over communism.

Since the publication of *Masters of Deceit* in 1958, I have been deeply gratified by the comments of many educators who said they found it useful as collateral reading on communism. Many of these educators pointed out the need for a second book which would highlight the contrasts between the freedom we enjoy and Communist totalitarianism, and have urged me to prepare one. This study of communism has been written in response to these numerous requests and in the hope that it will meet this need.

In providing the answers to some key questions about communism, this book is intended to serve only as a point of departure, a place from which one can journey into deeper understanding through additional reading and study. A free society depends for its vitality and strength upon the vigor and patriotism of its individual citizens. Knowledge of communism—the challenge of our age—and an appreciation of our American heritage will enable us to discipline ourselves for the hard decisions, the responsible judgments, the dedication, and the sacrifices which will have to be made to insure the continued existence of our nation and the perpetuation of freedom itself.

J. Edgar Hoover

May 25, 1962

Contents

Historical Materialism, Economic Determinism,
Communist Interpretation of History, Marx' Surplus
Value Theory, Inevitability of Communism,
Communism Is the Ultimate Stage, Communism Is
Not Scientific, Fallacies in Economic Determinism,
History Influenced by Many Factors, Communist
Morality, False Prophets

Part Three   Power Structure

Illustrations

Part One

Attractions

Chapter 1

All Things to All Men

An American citizen died in Moscow on September 1, 1961. It seemed especially appropriate that this particular man should have died in the Soviet Union, because he was William Z. Foster, for many years a leader of the Communist Party, USA, and a man who had dedicated the greater part of his adult life to the interests of the Soviet Union. Foster had gone to Moscow early in 1961 for the declared purpose of receiving medical treatment which, he claimed, he could not afford in the United States. When he died there at the age of 80, he held the title of chairman emeritus, or honorary chairman, of the Communist Party, USA.

As a fitting reward for Foster's long years of service to the Communist movement in the United States, officials of the Soviet Union offered to honor him by burial within the Kremlin walls. At the request of Foster's American comrades, however, Foster's remains were cremated. Before the ashes were flown to the United States, an impressive memorial ceremony for Foster was held in Moscow's Red Square. This was attended by many prominent officials of the Communist Party of the Soviet Union who paid tribute to the man who had served the Communist cause so well. Tributes to Foster from many other Communist parties throughout the world also poured in to the Communist Party, USA. At a ceremony on October 14, 1961, Foster's ashes were placed in a cemetery just outside Chicago.

Communists Are Dedicated

Foster's death did not signify any relaxation of Communist activities in the United States. If anything, it gave rise to a determination to intensify those efforts under the party's leader, Gus Hall, who, like Foster, has devoted his life to the Communist movement. The extent of Hall's dedication and the lengths to which he is prepared to go to achieve a Soviet America are best illustrated by his own words. In 1934, Hall, then a member of the party's youth group, the Young Communist League, was convicted of participating in a riot in Minneapolis, Minnesota. During his trial, the following exchange with Hall occurred:

Q. But you would prefer the Russian—you would prefer to be in Russia?

A. I prefer America with a Soviet government.

Q. And you are willing to fight and overthrow this government?

A. Absolutely.

Q. And you are willing to take up arms and overthrow the constituted authorities?

A. When the time comes, yes.

The dedication of men like Foster and Hall is, unfortunately, not an isolated thing. It is the trademark of a world movement seeking to conquer free men everywhere. That movement has been a threat since 1917, when Communists seized control of Russia. In the short period of time which has elapsed since then, the world Communist movement has built an empire. By the end of 1961, its leaders were able to boast of a world membership of some 40,000,000 in 87 Communist parties scattered throughout the world. Already in control of one-fourth of the territory of the world and one-third of the world's population, the members of this predatory movement are working to make a reality of the expressed desire of their leaders to see the Red Flag flying over every country in the world.

Most of us find it difficult, if not impossible, to understand how anyone who enjoys the rights and privileges of American citizenship—and the great majority of Communists in our country are either naturalized or native-born citizens—can bring himself to join a movement which is such an outspoken foe of our entire way of life. Why, we may ask, are people like Foster and Hall attracted to communism? Why do they want to see a Communist

U.S.S.R. AFTER WORLD WAR I

COUNTRIES OF COMMUNIST EMPIRE TODAY

1. ALBANIA
2. BULGARIA
3. CHINA
4. CUBA
5. CZECHOSLOVAKIA
6. EAST GERMANY
7. ESTONIA
8. HUNGARY
9. LATVIA
10. LITHUANIA
11. NORTH KOREA
12. NORTH VIET NAM
13. OUTER MONGOLIA
14. POLAND
15. RUMANIA
16. TIBET
17. U.S.S.R.
18. YUGOSLAVIA

United States? What factors do the Communists exploit to gain adherents to their cause? *Because it promises to cure all of the world's ills, communism has a universal attraction, but, in practice, it has proved to be an illusion.*

Promise as a Weapon

Communism claims to be a philosophy which explains the origin of man, his development, and his ultimate destiny. It confidently promises to bring about a world in which full equality, an abundance of the material benefits of life, and complete social justice will prevail. In short, communism claims to offer all things to all men. But, it does not stop there. Communism has also worked out a program of specific action in order to achieve its goals. Basically, therefore, communism appeals to people in terms of their universal needs and desires.

The breadth of its promise enables communism to exploit many factors which influence people's lives. Because human nature is so complex and because the various nations of the world differ so widely in the degree of their development, it is virtually impossible to single out any one factor as predominant in the Communist drive to gain additional supporters. Moreover, each individual is ordinarily moved to follow a specific course of action by a combination of motives. While it is possible that one motivating factor may be more important than another, the attraction of an individual to communism usually results from an interaction of several factors which the Communists have been able to exploit.

The Communist approach is a two-sided one with both a positive and a negative aspect. Negatively, communism attempts to create a deep-seated discontent with existing conditions in non-Communist nations. Positively, it offers a tempting challenge to all mankind to join forces in forging a world in which, communism claims, the exploitation of man by his fellow man will be forever ended.

In considering the reasons people are attracted to communism, we are fortunate in having available the experiences of many former members of the party who have rejected communism. The experiences of these former Communists in our own country and in other nations show that they joined the party for varied reasons. In most cases, it is impossible to single out any one specific reason or event and to say that it alone influenced a given individual to join the party. Generally, however, we can group the all-encompassing attractions of communism into four major classifications: *economic, sociological, political, and psychological.*

Economic Attraction

The economic attraction of communism is probably the best known and most easily recognized. During periods of economic depression and unemployment, many persons suffer great hardships. Faced with inadequate housing, mounting personal debts, perhaps even hunger, some lose all hope that the future will bring any improvement. In these desperate circumstances, some individuals are willing to accept desperate remedies. They become susceptible to Communist claims that all economic problems —unemployment, low wages, periodic depressions—are inherent capitalist ills but will automatically disappear under communism. Concerned only with eliminating the cause of poverty and hunger, they conclude that they have nothing to lose and everything to gain by rebelling against the prevailing economic order. Others, not necessarily the victims of poverty themselves, are susceptible to the economic attraction of communism because they sometimes see a wide disparity between their belief in the brotherhood and equality of all men and the inequities they observe. They see in communism, on the other hand, an elaborate blueprint for a perfect social order based on an economic theory which claims to be able to cure society of all its ills.

Sociological Attraction

The sociological attraction of communism is based on exploitation of social injustices and inequalities. Many of these are of a chronic nature and do not lend themselves to quick and easy solutions. For this reason, the sociological attraction of communism is more enduring than the economic, which loses much of its impact during periods of general prosperity. There are probably as many sociological attractions of communism as there are social problems throughout the world. To Communists, everyone who has been the victim of some form of social injustice or prejudice is a potential recruit for communism. In some cases, Communist membership is the result, not so much of any particular social problem or injustice, but of a general sense of frustration with existing conditions. In still other instances, the individual is attracted to communism by the desire to establish, for its own sake and apart from any motive of self-interest, a society in which all injustice has been eliminated. Some reformers, impatient with what they consider the slow process of achieving reforms under the democratic process, become convinced that social justice will be achieved only under communism. Communist propaganda exploits this dissatisfaction and frustration over sociological issues —both real and imagined—and portrays the Communist movement as the champion of social protest, the only force striving to improve the conditions of the oppressed.

Political Attraction

The political attraction of communism is based largely on the claim that all of the progress made by the Soviet Union within the comparatively short period since 1917 is due entirely to communism. Communist propaganda continually highlights Soviet economic, industrial, scientific, educational, and technological progress. However, no mention is made of the terrible price in human suffering and human lives which has been paid for transforming the Soviet Union into a world power.

If the Communist claim is accepted at face value, the political appeal of communism is apparent. No political system—not even democracy—provides any magic formula which will dispel all human ills. Faced with the imperfections of human nature, our free society makes no claim to be able to bring about a perfect world. Communism, on the other hand, promises not only a perfect political order but also an economic, social, and cultural paradise here on earth. Moreover, it offers an effective, tested organizational apparatus—the Communist party—which can be used to seize and wield political power.

Psychological Attraction

Many persons have joined the Communist party because the Communist movement appears to satisfy some basic psychological or emotional need. Communism affords a form of release to those who feel a sense of insecurity or inadequacy in their personal lives. It provides a retreat for those who cannot bear the responsibility of individual decision or action. In the party, all decisions are made by the party leaders for the individual. At the other extreme, the party also furnishes those possessed by the will for power the opportunity to dominate and exert authority over others. Still others find the Communist party a vehicle for expressing their resentment and hostility toward society. In some cases, broken homes resulting in the deterioration of parental authority and discipline have created personal conditions leading to the acceptance of communism by the young.

For some who have given up their religious faith, communism serves as a substitute for religion. Sheer boredom drives others in the direction of communism. They often turn to it as an escape from the humdrum routine of daily life, and the Communist movement fulfills their need for new activities and excitement. For those who have a desire to "do something," the party offers an almost endless round of meetings, educational classes, and opportunities to distribute propaganda, solicit contributions, and organize demonstrations. Before long, the individual loses himself in the Communist movement, becoming so involved in party affairs that he abandons all outside interests and makes the party his whole life.

The Communist movement has been able to exploit these and similar psychological impulses. Adherents to communism are constantly reminded that they are the most enlightened segment of society, the "vanguard" of the working class, and an elite leadership group whose duty it is to educate and guide the masses. Communist theory assures all Communists that the triumph of communism is inevitable and that they represent the "wave of the future." In so doing, it gratifies an urge to espouse a cause and to devote one's entire energies to it. Communism, like any other "cause," affords countless opportunities for selfless dedication and self-sacrifice.

Membership in the party gives one the feeling of being part of a disciplined and organized group which knows where it is going. The individual member can glory in the gains of the international Communist movement and is sustained by the belief in his own contribution to the inevitable progress of history and by the satisfaction found in merging his own personality and interests in the cause of "humanity." In many cases, communism, although an atheistic and materialistic ideology, stimulates in its members an excessive zeal which is fanatic in its intensity.

The reasons, then, that people accept communism are many and diverse. The four major ones we have discussed are by no means all-inclusive, nor are they always clearly defined and easily recognized. In most cases, party membership is based on more than one of these motives, and in every case the impact of these motives has been affected by specific experiences and events in the life of each party member. If there is a common denominator in all of these motives, it is that they all represent a protest against some aspect of existing conditions and a desire to change these conditions in some way.

Attraction for the Underdeveloped Nations

The four major attractions of communism—the economic, sociological, political, and psychological—are evident today in the underdeveloped nations of the world. Millions of people in these countries are living in ignorance and poverty. Many have an inadequate diet and are subject to diseases which could be prevented by the adoption of simple hygienic measures and improved living conditions. Many have little or no opportunity for education or technical training to improve their status in life and, frequently, the only jobs available to them are neither economically rewarding nor personally satisfying.

At the same time, people in other parts of the world are enjoying the benefits of modern civilization. Miracle drugs have virtually wiped out some diseases and act as effective deterrents to others. New methods and materials have spurred the construction of better housing. Automation is causing a revolution in industrial production. Rapid transportation methods now link whole continents closer together. Man has taken the first steps toward conquering outer space. The peaceful application of atomic energy holds forth the promise of even more spectacular achievements in the future.

Through widespread advances in communications, the people of the underdeveloped nations are becoming increasingly aware of the advantages enjoyed by others. Relatively dormant for centuries, they have suddenly awakened and are no longer resigned to low levels of social, economic, and political development. It is only natural that they should want to improve their own lives and to provide their children with an opportunity to live in a better world. Swept up in what has been described as the revolution of rising expectations, they are demanding results—not in terms of years—but immediately.

The revolution of rising expectations is not a Communist-inspired revolution. It is a natural reaction against poverty and misery which has been spurred by contacts with the more highly developed nations. Its basic premise is that, in this era of scientific and technical progress, it is no longer necessary for one-half of the world's people to live in poverty and misery.

Era of Rapid Social Change

We are living in a world of profound and rapid changes, revolutionary in a sense never before experienced by mankind. A series of simultaneous revolutions in science, technology, industry, and communications are taking place. Social transformations are the order of the day as governments rise and fall overnight and new nations, many of them insufficiently prepared, gain their independence.

The former colonial dependencies are faced with staggering problems. They are determined to create a modern industrial society overnight without going through the gradual transitional process from which, after centuries, the major industrial nations of the West emerged. The abrupt changes in the underdeveloped nations during the twentieth century will undoubtedly disrupt traditions as the people in these nations are torn between their reverence for the old and their admiration for the new. The problems facing these nations as they seek to become self-governing are indeed formidable. Typically, they lack a trained body of civil servants and a background or tradition of freedom. Educational and economic levels are often distressingly low. In areas where such conditions exist, there is the danger that some will view the totalitarian discipline of communism as the simplest and most efficient means of building a modern industrial nation.

Communism Exploits Nationalism

The Communists are doing their best to exploit the natural ferment which characterizes the underdeveloped nations at the present time. Every possible means is being used to convince

these countries that communism is the answer to all their problems. The Soviet Union is held up as tangible "proof" of the
possibility of quickly transforming agricultural nations into industrial powers. The Communists fan the flames of nationalism
and portray themselves as the strongest supporters of the right of
all nations to their complete independence. Offers of trade agreements; technical, economic, and military aid; and university
scholarships are showered on the underdeveloped nations.

At the same time, the Communist parties in these nations are
continuously working to undermine non-Communist governments. They realize that their conspiratorial organization is
ideally suited to gaining power during periods of turbulence
when weak non-Communist governments are particularly vulnerable to subversion or guerrilla warfare. Communists claim that
the triumph of communism is inevitable. They are fully aware,
however, that present-day conditions offer them their best practical opportunity and that as the newly formed nations resolve the
problems inherent in their transitions to independence, the
chances of a Communist seizure of power will decline.

This explains why the Communists are devoting so much of
their efforts to the underdeveloped nations. They claim that they
are working in harmony with the general trend of this revolutionary and visionary era. Yet, in attempting to superimpose
their counterfeit revolution on the legitimate and natural revolution of rising expectations, Communists are the parasites of the
modernization process.

Illusion and Reality

The attractions of communism are countered by the fact that
millions have abandoned the Communist movement in disgust.
No one word can accurately describe the feelings of these people.
If there were one such word, it would probably be *disillusionment.*
That disillusionment is a common characteristic of former Communists should not be surprising. When communism is studied
objectively from a philosophical, economic, political, or any other
point of view, the theory and practices of communism are found
to be basically false, impractical, and invalid. In other words,
communism proves to be in fact an illusion.

Stripped of its deception, the illusion of communism stands
exposed in all its brutality. It is no wonder that disillusionment

overcomes many once attracted to communism. The true nature of communism constitutes a repudiation of all they believed in and for which they made countless sacrifices. Those disillusioned by communism are dismayed at the wide gulf between Communist principles and Communist tactics, and are appalled by the difference between what communism promises and what it produces.

Where communism promises abundance, the disillusioned see hunger. They see tyranny, although communism promises freedom. They see brutality, thought control, oppression and human degradation where communism promised liberation, justice, and the development of a new Communist man in a better society. They see inhuman exploitation, not only of men, but of entire nations by a movement which pledges to end the exploitation of man by his fellow man.

Process of Disillusionment

The process of disillusionment with communism may begin with some personal experience or historical event. Among the personal experiences which have led to disillusionment with communism are visits to the Soviet Union, a distaste for party regimentation, resentment over the party's interference in personal affairs, suppression of all criticism within the party, incompetency and corruption of party leaders, and a sudden realization of the party's inherently subversive aims and illegal tactics.

Frequently, disillusionment with communism takes place as a result of some historical event which reveals to the member for the first time the true nature of world communism. The signing of the non-aggression pact between Germany and the Soviet Union in 1939, coming as it did after years of Communist propaganda attacks on Hitler and nazism, caused thousands of party members to leave in disgust. The Moscow purge trials during the 1930's shocked many party members out of their illusions about communism. Other events which have had a similar effect include Communist aggressions during and after World War II, the exposures of Communist-inspired espionage, the recitation of Stalin's crimes by Khrushchev, and the brutal suppressions of the uprisings in East Germany and Hungary.

Disillusionment with communism based on some dramatic personal experience or a definite historical event is usually clear-cut.

However, in many other cases, the process of disillusionment takes place slowly, almost imperceptibly, over a period of years. Some party members may have serious doubts regarding the validity of Communist theory at the very time they join the party, but, in one way or another, they manage to rationalize these doubts and temporarily explain them away. These members may eventually leave the party, but only after a period of doubt and inner conflict which sometimes lasts for years. Significantly, too, the final step of breaking the bond of total involvement with communism frequently causes a shattering crisis in the former member's personal life, and many are tormented for years after leaving the party trying to decide whether or not their decision was correct. This is particularly true of those who remained in the party for extensive periods of time or held important party positions. In these cases, the rejection of communism is not an easy step.

A lifelong party member, after years of sacrifice and effort, may have his own office and staff. He frequently has a wife and children to support. He has become accustomed to the applause and obedience of the rank-and-file members. His rejection of communism means giving up the job for which he has worked hard during the most productive years of his life and being thrown into the labor market to compete for a job at which he probably has not worked in years. In addition, there are even more important intangible considerations than the practical financial one. He will be branded, paradoxically, as a "traitor" and "stool pigeon" by his long-time associates in the party, and he will lose the feeling of power and importance which he enjoyed in the party. For a party member to reject communism, therefore, often involves a great number of complex emotional problems.

Yet, millions have rejected communism. The Communist dream of an ideal society has been proved a nightmare by the reality of life under communism. In no way has this been more graphically revealed than by the mass exodus of refugees from Communist nations, in many cases at considerable personal danger. From 1945 until 1962, some 10,000,000 persons, denied a meaningful ballot, voted in the only possible way—with their feet —and fled. The stream of refugees from the so-called workers' paradise of East Germany reached such proportions that the Communists were finally forced to erect the infamous wall across Berlin in an effort to halt the flow. The wall transformed East Germany into a massive concentration camp from which its inmates escaped only at the peril of their lives. It stands as a monument to the bankruptcy of Communist promises.

The reasons that these millions have fled communism are a ringing indictment of its failures. In some cases, the reason was the low standard of living. In others it was the lack of opportunity. Some people could not stand the restrictions on where and how they were to earn their living. Some left so that they could worship freely in accordance with their religious beliefs. With still others, it was to regain the right to think, act, and express themselves freely. Many objected to having the state rear and educate their children. Their flight is a massive rebellion against the gross inequities and cruelties they experienced under communism.

In the United States, many more people—literally tens of thousands—have passed through the doors of the Communist party than have seen fit to stay. The overwhelming majority of the persons who have been members of the Communist movement in this country have forsaken it, disillusioned by the failure of communism to live up either to their hopes or to its own promises.

Part Two

Origins

Chapter 2

Foundations of Modern Communism

One hundred years ago, communism was virtually unknown. Today, there is hardly a country in which its impact has not been felt. Phrases such as "cold war" and "Iron Curtain" have become part of our everyday vocabulary. Our government, from the taxes we pay, must spend billions of dollars each year on national defense to fortify ourselves and our allies against Communist aggression.

Why are we so concerned about communism? Why do we find it necessary to spend so much for defense? The answer to these questions is that Communists are committed to the destruction of our way of life and dedicated to the establishment of a world Communist society. This conflict with communism is not a struggle of our choosing. But, even though we did not start it, we cannot ignore it. We must win the struggle if freedom is to survive.

In any struggle, it is essential to know two things: what you are fighting *for* and what you are fighting *against*. If knowledge of the former is absent, the will to win will be lacking. If knowledge of the latter is absent, confusion and uncertainty will result. Therefore, in the struggle against communism, it is vital to know and to understand the full meaning of the freedom that we are fighting to preserve and to expand. It is equally vital to know and to understand what communism is and how it threatens freedom.

Communism Defined

A most important thing to know about communism is that there is a vast difference between what Communists say it is and what it actually is. An official definition, for example, was adopted at the Twenty-second Congress of the Communist Party of the Soviet Union in October, 1961, and reads as follows:

> Communism is a classless social system with one form of public ownership of the means of production and full social equality of all members of society; under it, the all-round development of people will be accompanied by the growth of the productive forces through continuous progress in science and technology; all sources of public wealth will gush forth abundantly, and the great principle 'From each according to his ability, to each according to his needs' will be implemented. Communism is a highly organised society of free, socially conscious working people in which public self-government will be established, a society in which labour for the good of society will become the prime vital requirement of everyone, a necessity recognised by one and all, and the ability of each person will be employed to the greatest benefit of the people.

This self-serving definition obviously portrays communism in an extremely favorable light. As will be shown in succeeding chapters, the following is an objective definition of communism:

> Communism (Marxism-Leninism) is the revolutionary, materialistic ideology used by its adherents to justify their efforts to seize power by any and all means for the forcible establishment of a world-wide totalitarian social order.

To understand communism as it exists today, we must trace the movement to its origin. In so doing, we will see that communism, as we know it today, represents a totalitarian form of socialism. *Karl Marx and Friedrich Engels developed the basic theoretical concepts which have evolved into communism as we know it today.*

Communism and Socialism Differ

Considerable debate has been occasioned by the use of the

terms communism and socialism. Each of these terms means different things to different people. Some use the words interchangeably. Even Communist propagandists frequently hail the triumph of socialism when they actually mean communism. In any study of communism, therefore, it is essential to distinguish between the terms.

Socialism is a general term which refers to a number of different, yet related, systems or doctrines. Its broad scope includes numerous points of view which, in some respects, differ sharply and fundamentally from each other. These systems differ not only in name, organization, and method, but, in some instances, also in the theoretical concepts on which they are based. Today, there are so many variations of Socialist thought that it probably would be impossible to offer a definition of socialism which would be acceptable to all of those who regard themselves as Socialists. Even Hitler's Fascist government, which ruled Germany from 1933 to 1945, was known as the National *Socialist* (Nazi) regime, and the initials U.S.S.R. mean, of course, the Union of Soviet *Socialist* Republics.

While various forms of socialism seek to restrict or eliminate private ownership of the means of production and distribution, they differ widely in the methods to be used to achieve their objectives. All appeal to workers for support. It is this competition for support of the same target group which explains why Communists and Socialists (who would appear, at first glance, to be natural allies) are, in many cases, bitter enemies.

The history of the two words, communism and socialism, helps to explain some of the confusion regarding the terms. The word socialism comes from the Latin word *socius,* which means an associate or an ally. It was used in Western Europe during the 1830's to refer to the views of those who believed that the interests of the individual should be subordinated to the welfare of society as a whole. The word communism is derived from the Latin *communis,* which means that which is common, e.g., the common people. In its political sense, communism means a society in which material goods are held and shared in common. The term first was used about 1840 to refer to the views of secret revolutionary societies which were then operating in Paris.

From the 1840's to the 1870's, Socialists were generally identified with the advocacy of the use of peaceful means to achieve their goals. Communists, on the other hand, were identified with the advocacy of the use of force and violence. However, between

1872 and 1917, the distinctions between the terms communism and socialism became blurred in the minds of most people. The word communism fell into disuse, and the word socialism was used almost exclusively in reference to the activities of the adherents of both views. This explains why the forerunner of what is now the Communist Party of the Soviet Union was known as the Russian _Social_ Democratic Labor Party until 1918. Today communism has come to mean the teachings of Karl Marx and Friedrich Engels as developed by V. I. Lenin and Joseph Stalin and interpreted, at times differently, by Nikita Khrushchev and Mao Tse-tung.

Socialism Defined

Even experts disagree as to precisely what socialism means. Yet, to understand its variation—communism—we need a working definition. For the purpose of this study of communism, therefore, the following broad definition of socialism will be used: _Socialism is the ownership by the state of the means of production and distribution._

In general, socialism would mean an end to private ownership of most forms of wealth and, instead, would substitute state ownership and control of wealth. Under a typical Socialist system, the government would own and operate public utilities, transportation and communication systems, banking facilities, and most, if not all, of the various manufacturing plants. It would direct the labor force and would regulate the distribution of practically everything produced. Under some variations of socialism, the government would also own the land. Obviously, for practical reasons, a society of this type demands some central planning authority with power to regulate and control production and distribution.

Distinguishing Types of Socialism

In general, there are two criteria for distinguishing the different variations of socialism. _First_, they may be distinguished by what they propose to do with the state (government organization). Under some forms of socialism, the state would be retained and its functions greatly expanded. Other variations of socialism (communism, for example) propose that the state be totally abolished. As we shall see, communism would substitute for the state a transitional dictatorship of the working class, which is eventually supposed to wither away. In practice, however, communism has evolved into a dictatorship of a self-appointed elite— a dictatorship that shows no signs of withering away.

Second, the variations of socialism may be distinguished through the means which each advocates to achieve its goal. Communism advocates the achievement of its goals by force and violence as in the Soviet Union. Other variations of socialism insist that it should be achieved only by peaceful, legal, and constitutional means.

Beginnings of Socialism

Socialism is not a new idea. The idea of sharing the material goods of life in common is probably as old as man himself. In the fourth century B.C., the Greek philosopher Plato wrote his famous work, *The Republic*. This book described a "perfect" state ruled by an intellectual class especially educated to carry out its duties. As pictured by Plato, this ruling class would hold no private property and would be subsidized by the rest of the population. In Western literature, Plato's "Republic" was the first major utopia—an imaginary society characterized by perfection— the fulfillment of mankind's dream of complete happiness on earth. The vision of, and the search for, a perfect society have persisted through the ages. Among the more famous descriptions of perfect societies are Sir Thomas More's *Utopia* (from which the term is derived), Tommaso Campanella's *City of the Sun*, Samuel Butler's *Erewhon* (an anagram of nowhere), and, in our own country, Edward Bellamy's *Looking Backward*.

Socialist ideas had found expression in Western Europe prior to the French Revolution in 1789 as a result of the economic upheavals which accompanied the Industrial Revolution earlier in the eighteenth century. These Socialist ideas, however, were largely of a moral-reform nature. Individual Socialists, lacking widespread popular support, had to limit themselves to denouncing the inequalities of the then existing society. The early Socialists stressed the importance of education, rather than revolutionary action, as the means of improving social conditions.

The French Revolution made no conscious attack on the right

of private property. In fact, one of its aims was to spread individual ownership to eliminate the inequalities which had prevailed under the feudal system. However, the development of industry which was taking place at the same time led to a linking of demands for political equality with demands for economic reform. Thus, for the first time, the differences between the rich and the poor developed into an active political struggle as well as an economic struggle.

It is impossible to select any specific date as the beginning of the modern Socialist movement. Even the French Revolution did not give rise to a fully developed Socialist movement. However, it did lay the groundwork for the long, drawn-out social struggles which were to erupt in Europe during the nineteenth century. In this sense, the French Revolution in 1789 may be said to mark the beginning of modern socialism.

Utopian Socialism

The French Revolution led some intellectuals to examine critically the capitalist system as its development was influenced by the progress of the Industrial Revolution. Dissatisfied with the obvious inequalities then existent under capitalism, they searched for means either to eliminate capitalism entirely or at least to alleviate the social, political, and economic injustices prevalent at the time. Their efforts gave rise to a school of Socialist thinkers led by Saint-Simon (1760–1825), Charles Fourier (1772–1837), and Louis Blanc (1811–1882). Karl Marx was highly critical of the solutions proposed by these "utopian" Socialists (as he described them). Nevertheless, he was influenced by them.

During the same period, other Socialists saw the need for more direct action. For example, Francois (Gracchus) Babeuf (1760–1797) was executed for organizing a secret society which unsuccessfully attempted to seize power in France. Babeuf's disciple, Louis Auguste Blanqui (1805–1881) also stressed the necessity for conspiratorial tactics and revolutionary methods. As we will discover later, Babeuf and Blanqui, in pioneering conspiratorial techniques, were forerunners of V. I. Lenin.

During the early nineteenth century, attempts were made to incorporate some of the utopian-Socialist ideas in model communities. Robert Owen (1771–1858), a successful Scottish textile manufacturer, lost a large part of his fortune trying to establish cooperative communities in Europe and in the United States. One of his experiments of this type took place at New Harmony, Indiana, during the 1820's, but was unsuccessful. Brook Farm, a cooperative community at West Roxbury, Massachusetts, was founded in 1841 and was based largely on the utopian ideals of the French Socialist, Charles Fourier. Nathaniel Hawthorne, famed American author, was a notable participant in this venture, which also ended in failure.

Utopian socialism had been based on appeals to morality, humanism, and justice. But such concepts were to lose all meaning and importance in the development of another Socialist theory that was to set the entire Socialist movement on a vastly different course. Based on a so-called scientific analysis of nature and history, it was described as "scientific socialism." Its originator, Karl Marx, claimed that his theory proved that the triumph of socialism was not only desirable, but inevitable.

Karl Marx—Founder of Modern Communism

Communism, as we know it today, can be said to have begun with the theories of Karl Marx. Marx was born May 5, 1818, and, as was the case with so many Socialist thinkers, had a middle-class background. His father had been a prosperous attorney in the town of Trier in the Rhineland section of Germany.

At a very early age, Marx demonstrated his intelligence and superior capacity for work. He attended the local high school at Trier and in 1835 entered the University of Bonn to study law. After a year at Bonn, he transferred to the University of Berlin. Here he concentrated more on history and philosophy than on law. It was while Marx was at the University of Berlin that he first came under the influence of the philosophy of Georg Wilhelm Friedrich Hegel (1770–1831). This influence was to have an impact upon the development of Marx' social theories.

Marx ultimately submitted his doctoral thesis to the University of Jena and was awarded the degree of Doctor of Philosophy in 1841. That same year, *The Essence of Christianity,* a criticism of religion by Ludwig Feuerbach (1804–1872), was published. Feuerbach was a materialist, and his philosophy subsequently had a great influence on Marx' intellectual development, for Marx had revealed an early interest in materialistic philosophy. His doctoral dissertation, for example, dealt with the differences between the materialistic philosophies of the Greek philosophers, Democritus and Epicurus. Moreover, Marx, in the foreword of his dissertation, indicated his hatred of all religious beliefs by including a quotation from Aeschylus' Prometheus: "In simple truth, I harbour hate 'gainst all the Gods."

Marx began contributing articles to, and subsequently edited, *Rheinische Zeitung*, a periodical in Cologne, Germany, but it was suppressed in 1843 because of its attacks on the Prussian government. The experience Marx gained as editor of this paper was an important factor in the development of his social theories, because it gave him an opportunity to observe at first hand the living and working conditions in Germany at that time. After the suppression of the periodical, Marx moved to Paris with his wife, the former Jenny von Westphalen, whom he had married that year. At that time, Paris was the center of Socialist thought, and Marx plunged immediately into an extensive study of socialism. Here he again met Friedrich Engels, whom he had first met in Germany in 1842. Their acquaintance later developed into a friendship which was to last their entire lives and which was to have a profound effect upon the lives of succeeding generations.

Engels, the son of a successful textile manufacturer, was born in Barmen, Germany, on November 28, 1820. After military service in the Prussian Army, he moved to Manchester, England, in 1842, to work at a textile factory in which his father was a partner. Here he came to know the long hours, low wages, hazardous working conditions, and child labor characteristic of the early stages of the Industrial Revolution.

The Communist Manifesto

In 1845, as a result of pressure brought by the Prussian government, Marx was ordered to leave France. He moved to Brussels, Belgium, where he was joined by Engels. The two men came into even closer contact with the industrial labor force, and in 1847 joined the League of the Just, a secret organization with headquarters in London. The League of the Just changed its name to the Communist League later that year and commissioned Marx and Engels to draw up a definitive statement of its aims and program. Marx and Engels agreed, and the *Communist Manifesto* was published under their joint authorship. Although published in 1848, this explosive, revolutionary, social document has remained the credo of the world Communist movement down to the present time. The *Manifesto* outlines in general terms many of the basic doctrines which Marx and Engels had developed, and concludes with this ringing call to arms:

> The Communists disdain to conceal their views and aims.
> They openly declare that their ends can be attained only
> by the forcible overthrow of all existing social conditions.
> Let the ruling classes tremble at a Communist revolution.
> The proletarians have nothing to lose but their chains.
> They have a world to win.
> Workingmen of all countries, unite!

In 1850, a dispute arose among the leaders of the Communist League and Marx transferred its headquarters to Cologne, Germany, where he had a group of adherents. This meant, in effect, the end of the Communist League, although it actually continued in existence until 1852, when its members in Cologne were tried and imprisoned.

Marx Finds Refuge in England

Shortly after the publication of the *Manifesto*, a revolution broke out in France and soon spread to Germany. Marx and Engels returned briefly to Paris and then proceeded to Cologne, where they organized a daily newspaper. As a result of inflammatory articles against the Prussian government, Marx was tried for sedition, but acquitted. In May, 1849, the Prussian government expelled him from Germany. After a brief stay in Paris, Marx secured political refuge in London, where he remained for most of the rest of his life. Engels, after taking part in the unsuccessful revolution in Germany in 1849, followed Marx to England.

During the early years of life in England, Marx and his family lived in dire poverty, plagued by creditors, sickness, squalor, and hunger. At times the children could not leave the house because they did not have shoes or suitable clothing, and Marx' wife became emotionally disturbed because of the wretched conditions under which they were compelled to live. Of their six children (the seventh was born dead), only three girls grew to maturity. The only period during which Marx had any type of steady employment was from 1852 until 1861, when he served as a foreign correspondent for the *New York Tribune*. Despite the hardships his studying and writing imposed upon his family, Marx, because he received frequent financial assistance from Engels, was able to devote his life to the development of his social and economic theories.

The First International

In 1864, the International Working Men's Association (also known as the First International) was organized at a conference in London, and Marx soon became its intellectual leader. The goal of the First International was to promote working-class unity, and its program, written by Marx, emphasized practical issues and ended with the words "workingmen of all countries, unite!"—the final cry of the *Communist Manifesto*.

Since the International eventually included representatives of most shades of Socialist thought in Western Europe, along with English trade unionists, its life was characterized by an almost continuous series of internal rivalries and disputes. Despite this internal dissension, however, the First International gradually grew in size and influence. Marx remained one of the leaders of the First International until 1872, when his leadership was challenged. Marx transferred the headquarters of the First International from London to New York in 1872. This, in effect, meant the death of the First International, which held its last congress in Philadelphia in 1876.

Das Kapital

From the time of his arrival in England, Marx had been concentrating on the economic aspects of his theory, making use of the extensive material available in the library of the British Museum. By the early part of 1858, Marx had decided to prepare a comprehensive analysis of the entire capitalist system. His disputes with other Socialists, however, and his activities in the First International delayed its publication until 1867, when the first volume of *Das Kapital* (Capital) was published. In the *Communist Manifesto*, Marx and Engels had outlined their theory of the struggle between opposing classes in society. In *Das Kapital*, Marx attempted, in a lengthy and tortuous argument, to explain his views of "capitalist exploitation" of the "working class."

Yet even with the publication of *Das Kapital*, Marx, to his disappointment, remained relatively unknown in England. The bitterness resulting from his personal life appeared, at times, to spill over into his writings and led to a running feud with other Socialists. In addition, Marx was a vain and domineering person who scorned and ridiculed everything and everyone with whom he disagreed. As a result, his circle of personal associates grew steadily narrower in his declining years.

Disappointed in the apathy of the English working class, Marx began studying conditions in the United States, where a series of financial crises had begun in 1873. He foresaw in America the highest development of capitalism in the shortest possible time, and, following his own theory, he was led to the erroneous conclusion that the United States would be one of the first nations to achieve communism.

Meanwhile, Marx' health, which had never been good, grew steadily worse. He had suffered from a liver condition, and his long, irregular hours, combined with a poor diet during his early years in England, were beginning to take their toll. He also developed a respiratory ailment. His long-suffering wife had developed cancer, of which she died in 1881. Marx spent the following year traveling to Algiers and to France in an effort to regain his health. He returned to London, following the death of his eldest daughter, and died there on March 14, 1883. His friend and collaborator, Engels, delivered the eulogy at Marx' burial at Highgate cemetery in London, where his grave is still maintained.

It was left to Engels to edit the final two volumes of *Das Kapital*, which Marx had left unfinished at his death, and those were finally published in 1885 and 1894. Engels briefly visited the United States and Canada in 1888. On his death on August 5, 1895, Engels left most of his estate to Marx' children.

The Second International

In 1889, six years before Engels' death, the Second International was organized in Paris. It was a loosely organized federation of workers' organizations which was nominally based on the views of Marx and Engels. Its program stressed the class struggle, the nationalization of industry, and the international solidarity of the working class. Engels encouraged the Marxists to participate in the Second International, anticipating that they would eventually control it. Contrary to his expectations, however, control of the Second International fell into the hands of a group of German Socialists who had abandoned Marx' revolutionary program and who were advocating that socialism be achieved by working within the framework of the capitalist system. The Second International developed into an influential organization in Western Europe, and many of its members served in the parliaments of such nations as England, France, and Germany. When World War I broke out in 1914, the majority of the Socialist parties supported their own governments, rather than the principle of the international solidarity of the working class. The Second International never recovered from the split which resulted.

Importance of Marx and Engels

Marx and Engels provided the theoretical foundations of the modern Communist movement. They selected aspects of German philosophical thought, English economic theory, and French Socialist ideas, modified them, adapted them, added some ideas of their own, and wove together a theory which they claimed was based on a "scientific" analysis of nature and history. This theory offers to its followers an explanation for the origin and development of the universe, a code of morality and ethics, an analysis of the direction of history, and a program of practical political activity. It promises a world-wide society in which the exploitation of man by his fellow man will be forever ended. In addition, by their emphasis on the class struggle and the necessity for revolutionary action, Marx and Engels generated within the over-all Socialist movement a revolutionary zeal and a driving force which, until their time, it had lacked. The seed they planted in Western Europe a little over a century ago, nourished by V. I. Lenin, has grown into the international Communist movement of today.

Chapter 3

Basic Communist Concepts

Communist theory plays a vital role in the life of every Communist party member. During their participation in the movement, Communists undergo a never-ending course of indoctrination. All Communist parties issue discussion guides and detailed study outlines dealing with Communist theory for the use of their members. Various types of party schools, many of them conducted secretly, are established in non-Communist countries, including our own, to teach individual party members the basic tenets of communism.

Non-Communists should have, at the very least, a general understanding of Communist theory. The fact that theory plays such an important role in the lives of Communists makes a general understanding of it mandatory if effective counteraction is to be taken against communism.

The theories of Marx and Engels are complex, but there are certain basic concepts which can be identified, examined, and evaluated to provide insight into Communist beliefs and action.

An evaluation of Communist doctrine is extremely important inasmuch as Communists are adept at citing historical events and phenomena which, at first glance, tend to support their beliefs, while ignoring facts and events which disprove these beliefs.

Communist theoreticians are compelled to do this because their arguments are based on false premises.

Communism has three underlying theoretical concepts: (1) a philosophy which is materialistic; (2) a method called the dialectic; and (3) an application of this philosophy and method to history and social developments (historical materialism).

Communist Concept of Materialism

Communists hold a *materialistic* philosophy. They believe that whatever man does, thinks, or feels can be explained in terms of dynamic matter alone, and that matter is the only thing that exists. They deny the existence of any spiritual being.

Communists claim that matter is self-sufficient—self-developing and self-perpetuating—and that there is no Supreme Being, or God, responsible for either the creation or the preservation of the universe.

Communists allege that man does not have a spiritual soul destined for immortality and that he is not essentially distinct from other forms of life.

Communists conclude that all religions and all moral codes derived from spiritual concepts are based on fantasy.

In adopting their materialistic interpretation, Communists assert that there is no essential difference between man and other forms of life. Man is merely the product of chemistry and physics, differing from the other forms of life only in the degree of his development. Therefore, Communists argue, since there is no Supreme Being, any moral law or code based on spiritual concepts is invalid.

Communists have a ready answer when challenged to explain why religious concepts have had such a profound effect upon civilization since the dawn of time. They say that primitive man devised a Supreme Being in order to account for the violent forces of nature and to justify his own inability to explain the unknown. This Being served as someone to whom primitive man could pray and offer sacrifices for deliverance from such occurrences as thunder and lightning, earthquakes, volcanic eruptions, tornadoes, and tidal waves. From this early beginning, Communists say, fixed patterns of prayer and other forms of worship developed, and religion became an important part of man's life.

Communists then explain that the "ruling class" exploits religious beliefs in order to preserve its privileged position in society. It is able to do so, Communists claim, because religion teaches such virtues as brotherly love, forgiveness, meekness, and resignation to one's fate with the promise of a supernatural life of eternal happiness. In following such teachings, Communists say, the poor and oppressed remain passive in the face of exploitation by the "ruling class." Therefore, Communists subscribe to the theory expressed by Marx that religion is "the opium of the people."

Communist Concept Refuted

Philosophers who disagree with the materialist view deny that man can be completely explained by such materialistic factors as organic operations, physiological functions, and physical sensations. They insist that ideals, thoughts, and inspirations are a part of man's nature and cannot be explained in terms of matter alone. These attributes are obviously spiritual, not material. Philosophers who are non-materialists reason that since man performs both spiritual and material functions, it necessarily follows that he is a spiritual as well as a material being.

Bound by materialistic theory, Communists do not acknowledge that motion in matter, or the very existence of matter itself, requires a source outside of matter. Non-materialist philosophers point out that Communists do not explain the origin of matter or the ultimate cause of motion in matter. The ultimate explanation of the existence of matter and of motion in it, according to non-materialist philosophers, can only be the existence of a Creator or Mover of the universe, usually called the Supreme Being, or God.

There are other factors to consider in the argument against the materialism of Communists. For example, millions of men have been guided for centuries by moral codes based on spiritual values. There has been widespread acceptance of the religious principles that teach kindness, love of neighbor, charity, justice, and the Golden Rule in contrast to the number who have scorned or rejected such principles. Could so many throughout the world down through the centuries have been so completely deceived?

Far from being an opiate, as Communists claim, religion has been and is today a dynamic force in the lives of men. Belief in an eternal reward in the next life does not preclude a striving for temporal rewards in this one. While most religions teach that it may not be possible to create a paradise on earth, they do encourage man to improve his status.

Man's achievements in such fields as politics, science, art, religion, and education, to mention just a few, illustrate the absurdity of Communist efforts to prove that man is not essentially different from other forms of life. Communism sweeps away from human experience all the great ideals for which man has struggled through the centuries. In practice, communism makes man's highest aspirations for the ideals of truth, justice, love, and honor merely illusions. Communism reduces man to an animal whose only destiny is to help fulfill the latest five-, seven-, or twenty-year plan.

The Dialectical Method

The word "dialectic" is derived from the Greek *dialektike,* meaning the art of discourse, reasoning, and debate. In ancient times, dialectics was the art of arriving at a truth through the clash of opposing views and arguments. Through such debate, opponents sought to highlight the contradictions in each other's arguments in order to arrive at a conclusion that contained the truth and avoided the errors in each position.

The dialectical method consists of three elements: the *thesis,* which is a positive concept or force; the *antithesis,* which is an opposing concept or force; and the *synthesis,* which is a new idea or force produced by the clash of the opposites inherent in the thesis and antithesis, and combining the best characteristics of both of them. The dialectical method is usually illustrated by means of the following diagram:

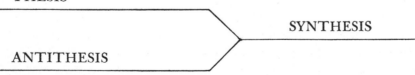

THESIS

ANTITHESIS

SYNTHESIS

The synthesis produced by the dialectic becomes a new thesis against which a new antithesis develops. Then the process begins anew to produce another synthesis.

Dialectical Materialism

Karl Marx combined the materialistic concept of the universe with the dialectical method. It will be recalled that the ideas of the German philosopher Hegel were influential in the development of Marx' theory. Hegel had applied the method of the dialectic in an attempt to explain the nature of the universe through a theory of historical development and progress. However, Hegel was an idealist. His philosophy is based on the concept that the universe is rational and spiritual. Marx rejected Hegel's views but borrowed the dialectical method and used it for his materialistic—as opposed to Hegel's idealistic—philosophy.

However, Marx went much further than Hegel in the use of the dialectic. Hegel had used the method to interpret the past and the present. Marx, working with Engels, applied it not only to explain the past and the present but also to predict the future. To them, it represented a means of understanding the past and a guide to practical action for both the present and the future.

The Communists believe the dialectical method enables them to understand the "general laws of development," not only of nature, but also of history. They believe that by applying this method to society they can analyze the past history of man, understand his present social relations, and foresee the future development of society.

The Communists claim that there are three "laws" which govern the operation of the dialectic. These laws are (1) *the law of the unity and struggle of opposites,* (2) *the law of negation, and* (3) *the law of the sudden leap.*

The Law of the Unity and Struggle of Opposites

According to the law of the unity and struggle of opposites, there is an inherent contradiction existing in all matter which drives it to further development. In support of this law, Communists cite the positive and negative charges of electricity, the breakdown of atoms into protons and electrons, the continuous change within the human body itself as cells are formed and die, and, in the social order, the contradiction between what Marx and Engels regarded as opposing classes. Communists claim that matter in motion is not a haphazard process but one which continually progresses toward a higher stage of development.

The Law of Negation

The second law of dialectical materialism is the law of negation. According to this law, the process of development necessarily entails the progress of everything in motion toward its own negation. Referring to the diagram on page 33, for example, it will be seen that the thesis is negated by the antithesis, and thus produces the synthesis. In turn, the synthesis becomes a new thesis against which a new antithesis arises. In the continuing process, each step is said to represent a higher stage of development.

Communists use the law of negation to explain the numerical increase or reproduction of things. The original object ceases to exist, as such, even though it may multiply or develop in the process. A seed ceases to exist, for example, when it germinates and develops into a plant. The plant developed as a result of the negation of the seed. The plant grows, flowers, is pollinated, and produces additional seeds, after which the original plant dies or is negated. However, the process has provided for additional plants.

In the process of development, Communists say, only what has become obsolete is negated. All that is good remains and develops progressively from lower to higher stages. Applying the law of negation to the social order, Communists theorize that feudalism was negated by capitalism which, in turn, will be negated by communism, with each stage discarding the obsolete of the prior stage and retaining only the good aspects in the developing dialectical process.

The Law of the Sudden Leap

The third law of dialectical materialism is the law of the sudden leap. According to this law, a series of *quantitative* changes frequently produces a *qualitative* change. Communists cite the example of water changing form to become either ice or steam. Adding heat to water in increasing amounts (quantitative changes) will, at a certain point (temperature), produce an abrupt transformation (sudden leap) of the water into steam (qualitative change). Conversely, the removal of heat from water by degrees will result in another sudden leap when the water becomes ice.

Dialectical materialism insists that *both* a series of gradual quantitative changes and a sudden leap are required for the emergence of new forms. But, while a series of quantitative changes precedes the emergence of new forms, the actual emergence is always the result of a sudden leap.

Using such a line of reasoning, Communists attempt to explain the development of man. They argue that inanimate objects underwent a series of quantitative changes and developed into living organisms as the result of a sudden leap. Subsequently, they say, animals became men after another series of quantitative changes had, through a sudden leap, produced the human mind. Communists, in applying this reasoning to the social order, describe revolution as the sudden leap which ushers in a new form of society.

Fallacies of Dialectical Materialism

Communists claim that the dialectical method of reasoning is superior to any other form of logic and that the relationship between it and other forms of logic is analogous to the relationship between higher mathematics and simple arithmetic. Upon analysis, however, the so-called laws which govern the operation of the dialectic do not *explain* anything. The law of the unity and struggle of opposites presupposes that matter is in motion. It does not *explain* the cause of this motion. Non-materialist philosophers hold that the ultimate explanation of the motion in matter is the existence of a Mover who transcends the universe, or God. The Communists admit that matter in motion is not a haphazard process but they insist that the order which exists in the universe is due solely to necessity in nature and not to any Supreme Lawgiver.

The law of negation and the law of the sudden leap, the other two laws which govern the operation of the dialectic, do not *explain* anything either. They merely describe occurrences which are apparent. It is common knowledge that a plant reproduces by developing seeds before it dies (negation) and that, by adding heat to water, it will, at a certain temperature, turn into steam (sudden leap). Merely describing these observable facts of nature, as the Communists do, does not *explain* them.

Despite its lack of validity, however, an understanding of dialectical materialism is vitally important to non-Communists, because it is more than just a set of abstract theoretical concepts.

For the Communists, dialectical materialism also serves as a working guide to practical action both in the present and for the future.

Historical Materialism

Communists interpret history as a materialistic process in which the dynamic factor is the class struggle. According to the *Communist Manifesto:*

> The history of all hitherto existing society is the history of class struggles.
> Freeman and slave, patrician and plebeian, lord and serf, guildmaster and journeyman, in a word, oppressor and oppressed, stood in constant opposition to one another, carried on an uninterrupted, now hidden, now open fight, a fight that each time ended, either in a revolutionary reconstitution of society at large, or in the common ruin of the contending classes.

This interpretation, known as historical materialism, is the result of the application by Communists of the theory of dialectical materialism to the history of man and society.

In developing the theory of historical materialism, Marx and Engels began with the idea that self-preservation is the first law of existence. It is this idea that governs all human relations, they said, and it is the common end which, in one way or another, all men pursue. Since the pursuit of this goal basically involves the production of the necessities of life, they concluded that the means of production constituted the fundamental force in history.

Economic Determinism

Marx and Engels declared that the nature of a society at any given time was the direct result of the means of production then in effect. They arrived at this conclusion by defining the means of production as the substructure of a society. Things such as the state, law, morality, and culture they identified as the superstructure. The substructure determines the superstructure, they declared, because the latter, either consciously or subconsciously, evolves from man's efforts to arrive at a means of producing and distributing the necessities of life with the least possible hindrance. This aspect of historical materialism is generally called *economic determinism.*

Marx and Engels distinguished two factors involved in producing the necessities of life. They identified the first factor as the productive forces—workers, their tools, and raw materials. The second factor, they said, was man's relationship in production—the relations between master and slave or capitalist and worker.

In the early primitive-communal societies, Marx and Engels said, relations between men were peaceful and harmonious because the means of production were owned in common. Gradually, however, through barter and trade among themselves and with other primitive communities, certain individuals acquired private ownership of the means of production. This created a change in the productive relations which, ever since, have been relations between directly opposing classes. In the struggle, the ruling class (those who own the means of production) live a life of luxury and ease, imposing the working conditions and setting the wages for the exploited class. The continuous clash of interests between the two opposing classes, Marx and Engels claimed, was responsible for all historical progress.

Marx and Engels thus concluded that the ultimate cause of all social upheavals is economic. They said that, when a new means of production is devised in the substructure of society, a conflict arises because the old superstructure is outmoded and the exploited class finally revolts against the existing social order. At first sight, this revolution appears to be a political struggle, since it is directed against the state—the most important element in the superstructure of society. But the fact that it was based on a change in the means of production, Marx and Engels said, makes it basically an economic change.

Communist Interpretation of History

Using the theory of historical materialism, Communists offer the following interpretation of all human history. Since the end of the early primitive-communal society, all succeeding societies have contained within themselves a "unity and struggle of opposites." This, it will be recalled, is the first law of the dialectic. It is represented by the opposing classes in society which have conflicting interests based upon their relationship to the means of production. As the conflict between them is intensified in the class struggle, the old society is negated and, through a sudden leap, is replaced by a new, higher form of society. The law of negation is, of course, the second law of the dialectic, and the law of the sudden leap is the third. This Communist interpretation of history may be likened to a spiral staircase.

At the base of the staircase, Communists claim, is the primitive-communal society. In it, the means of production consisted of clubs and similar primitive weapons and tools. The members of this society were forced to band together for subsistence and protection because of the low level of development of the means of production. At this stage, common ownership of the means of production prevented any "exploitation of man by man."

Men learned gradually to forge metals and manufacture tools, such as axes, plows, and shovels. Agriculture and various handicrafts became specialized skills. To some degree, labor became specialized. Through barter and trade, private ownership of the means of production emerged.

The early primitive-communal system developed into the next higher step—slavery. This system was characterized by private ownership not only of the means of production but also of the workers, or slaves, themselves. One section of society, the slave-owners, completely dominated the other, the slaves, and thus divided society into two antagonistic classes.

At this point, Communist theory becomes extremely vague regarding any major change in the means of production which brought about the downfall of the slave society and ushered in the feudal system. The Communist textbook, *Fundamentals of Marxism-Leninism,* which was prepared in the Soviet Union, attempts to hide the defect in the following way:

> But the time came when the possibilities of progress inherent in the slave mode of production were exhausted. . . . More and more insistently the needs of the development of the productive forces demanded the abolition of the old production relations.
> . . . In the end, under the combined blows of the uprisings of the working classes and the attacks of neighbouring barbarian tribes, which the slave-owning state, weakened by internal contradictions and conflicts, could no longer resist, the slave system crumbled. . . .

According to Communist theory, the class struggle in the feudal system was more intense than it had been in the slave society. At

COMMUNIST VIEW OF HISTORY

COMMUNISM

CAPITALISM

FEUDALISM

SLAVERY

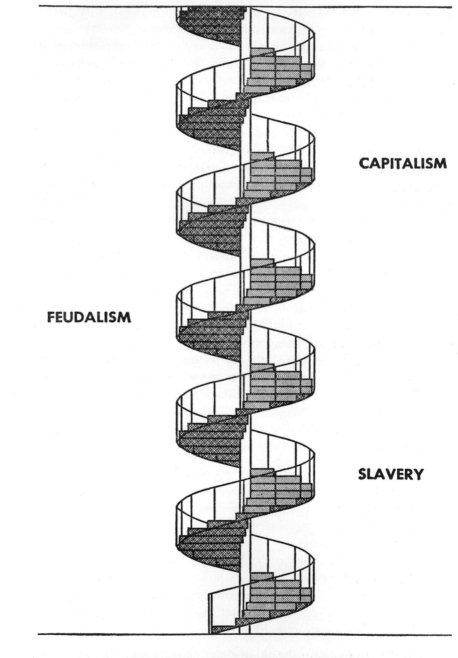

PRIMITIVE-COMMUNAL SOCIETY

the same time, the advances brought about by the Industrial Revolution of the eighteenth and nineteenth centuries led to the establishment of large manufacturing plants based on craft techniques and created a new class. This class was the bourgeoisie which operated the new factories—the new means of production. The resulting struggle between the feudal lords and the rapidly growing bourgeoisie, with whom were allied the workers and the serfs who had gained their freedom from serfdom, brought about the leap from feudalism to capitalism.

Capitalism is the fourth phase in the Communist view of history. Again, under this phase, the pattern for relations between classes in society allegedly is determined by the method of production. The owners of the means of production, the capitalist class (bourgeoisie), exploit the wage earners (proletariat). Because the latter group does not own the means of production, it has only its labor power to sell.

Marx' Surplus Value Theory

In analyzing capitalist society, Karl Marx developed what is usually referred to as the *surplus value theory*. It was based on several economic theories which were popular in the early nineteenth century but are now completely discredited. Basic in Marx' theory is the premise that the value of any commodity depends upon the amount of labor required to produce it. This premise was known as the labor theory of value.

Working from the idea that labor alone produces value, Marx reasoned that the profits of capitalists could come only from productive time for which workers were not paid. According to this view, although labor determines value, those who labor do not receive full payment for the value of the goods their labor produces, and the capitalists keep the "surplus value" for themselves as profit. Marx claimed that this "surplus value" was, in reality, stolen from the workers.

The limitations of the Communist theory of value are obvious. It completely eliminates, in determining value, any contributions from the investment of capital, the ingenuity or competence of management, and the application of talent or technical and scientific refinements in the means of production. The theory of surplus value cannot explain, for example, why a painting by Rembrandt will sell for more than $2,000,000, a price far exceeding that paid for the most expensive automobile, which certainly required much more labor to produce.

Inevitability of Communism

Despite its absurdity as an economic principle, the theory of surplus value serves Communists by justifying the eventual triumph of the proletariat over capitalism as the triumph of good over evil. Using this theory, Marx and Engels argued that the concentration of the means of production in huge factories employing thousands of workers gave production a social character, meaning that the worker no longer produced individually but in conjunction with countless other workers. At the same time, they said, the value of what was being produced was not being distributed to society as a whole, but was accruing only to the small group owning the means of production. As the competition for profits intensified among the capitalists, more and more of them would be forced into the ranks of the working class. As the capitalist class grew smaller and smaller, there would be an accumulation of more and more capital into fewer and fewer hands. This eventually would result in the development of monopolies, cartels, and trusts.

Marx and Engels claimed that the entire system contained within itself the seeds of its own destruction. As the number of capitalists dwindled and the number of workers increased, the swelling ranks of the latter would suffer still greater exploitation as the remaining capitalists continued to increase their profits at the expense of laborers. The increasing severity of the exploitation would force workers to unite to protect themselves, and thereby create the very force which ultimately would destroy the entire capitalist system. Marx and Engels described it as follows:

> . . . What the bourgeoisie, therefore, produces, above all, is its own grave diggers. Its fall and the victory of the proletariat are equally inevitable. . . .
> The weapons with which the bourgeoisie felled feudalism to the ground are now turned against the bourgeoisie itself.
> But not only has the bourgeoisie forged the weapons that bring death to itself; it has also called into existence the men who are to wield those weapons—the modern working class—the proletarians.

The entire Communist view of history, as we have seen, is related directly to the idea of class struggle which Marx and Engels developed. All history, according to them, is the history of warfare between classes, and it is this class warfare which produces change. In the Communist view of the capitalist system, the power of the so-called exploiting class is protected by the capitalist state. No matter what form the capitalist state may take, such as a democracy, a republic, a dictatorship, or a monarchy, its purpose, according to Communists, is to perpetuate the oppression of the working class. Therefore, the working class must smash the government of the ruling class and crush any resistance on the part of the capitalists. Once the workers have destroyed the capitalist state or government by revolution, and have become themselves the ruling class, they can proceed to construct the fifth phase in the historical development of society—communism.

Communism Is the Ultimate Stage

Communism is the ultimate phase of historical materialism. But in the process of reaching this final stage, Communists say, it is necessary to pass through a lower phase—their version of state socialism. In this phase, Communists say, man will be guided by the principle "from each according to his ability, to each according to his work." This allegedly is the stage of development that has been achieved in the Soviet Union.

Communists claim that, when the stage of communism is reached, the means of production will be owned by all the people, and the exploitation of man by his fellow man will have ended. Since there will be no private ownership of the means of production, they say, there will be a classless society. In it, all forms of the state (the instrument of one class against another), then unnecessary, will have withered away.

The Communist vision of a classless society of necessity assumes that the dialectical process will cease to operate in the area of man's social development. Man's character will change, according to Communist theory, once his economic activities are no longer motivated by self-interest. Thus a new man—the Communist man—will emerge in a Communist society in which no distinction will be made between mental and physical labor and in which material abundance, absolute equality, and true social justice will prevail.

It is obvious, however, that the assumption of a cessation of the dialectical process contradicts the claim that communism is a theory of progress, since it would lead to a completely static society in which all incentive for further progress would be eliminated. Moreover human history demonstrates that every complex society has required, if nothing else, some individual or group of individuals with authority over its other members. Otherwise, the result would be anarchy. Because every individual has different talents and abilities, there never has been, nor can there ever be, a society without differences—a classless society.

Even in the Soviet Union, where the Communists have held power since 1917 and have eliminated private ownership of the means of production, there is no evidence that a classless society is evolving. It is a well-known fact that there is a wide disparity between the economic status and the privileges of the Communist hierarchy and the average citizen. This is equally true in all of the other Communist countries. This situation was well described by Milovan Djilas, former vice president of Yugoslavia, in his book *The New Class,* which depicts the emergence of a new ruling class—the Communist party officialdom.

Communists declare that communism must, of necessity, be world-wide. They state that the existence of capitalist nations anywhere in the world requires nations working toward communism to retain their state organizations and their military forces. Only when communism has conquered the entire world and eliminated class struggle, they say, can there be real peace and harmony in the world. Under pure communism, they assert, society will be based on the principle "from each according to his ability, to each according to his needs."

Communism Is Not Scientific

The theory of historical materialism, with its emphasis on economics, at first glance may seem to present a logical interpretation of history. It may appear to offer a solution for social inequities. But the truth is that it is only a superficial description of a few historical occurrences which have been carefully selected to support the theory. It does not offer a consistent and plausible explanation for all historical events.

The theory of historical materialism was conceived by Marx and Engels during a period of the Industrial Revolution when there were great social inequities and a marked difference in economic classes. This theory attempts to deal with all history in the light of the peculiar and temporary conditions of that particular era. For this reason, historical materialism falls far short of the Communists' claims that it is a "science" of history.

Even a cursory examination of the Communist theory of history points up its invalidity. There are no factual grounds for the assumption in the dialectical interpretation that all history represents continuous progress toward a higher stage of development. On the contrary, any rational analysis of history must admit that all historical developments are not necessarily forward or progressive. Some have been steps backward; for example, the Nazi regime which, as a matter of state policy, committed monstrous atrocities against Jews.

The theory of historical materialism also fails to explain the existence of another society which does not fit into the Communist five-stage sequence of development. This was the Asiatic or Oriental society. Unlike Western society, which is based on private ownership of the means of production, the Asiatic society was based on state ownership of the means of production. In this despotic society there were two main classes, an all-powerful state bureaucracy and the masses. The latter class was largely devoid of power. The Asiatic society never went through the feudal era, and it was notable for the absence of class revolutions.

Marx was aware of the Asiatic society, because he specifically distinguished between "the Asiatic, the ancient, the feudal, and the modern bourgeois modes of production as so many epochs in the progress of the economic formation of society." However, because the Asiatic society cannot be fitted into the Communist theory of history as a spiral staircase of progress toward communism, references to this society usually are suppressed now in Communist literature. Ironically, the despotic Asiatic society, with its all-powerful state bureaucracy and its masses largely devoid of power, was strikingly similar to the society which is developing in the Soviet Union.

Fallacies in Economic Determinism

Economic determinism—the theory that the nature of society at any given time is the direct result of the means of production then in effect—is the key to the theory of historical materialism.

However, it fails to explain why each of the societies of ancient Greece and Rome experienced a variety of essentially different forms of government ranging from despotism to democracy, despite the fact that slavery was the means of production in both countries. Applying the theory of economic determinism to the United States also demonstrates that it is not scientific. This country has had the same form of government since the Constitution was adopted, yet the means of production have not been constant in all parts of our nation. During the course of our history, we have experienced production under slavery, as well as under highly developed capitalism. It is obvious that the nature of any society is dependent upon the interplay of many factors besides the means of production. Among these other factors are such variables as climate, geographical location, natural resources, customs, religions, languages, traditions, density of population, and neighboring peoples.

Oversimplification in the concept of historical materialism is not limited to economic determinism. This defect also applies to the Communist theory regarding the class struggle. Contrary to Communist belief, any given society is never broken down into just two opposing classes. Even Marx conceded the existence of a middle class made up of the owners of small businesses, professionals, salesmen, accountants, and skilled artisans. Marx contended that this middle class would be forced into the proletariat by the monopolistic practices of the capitalists. But the history of the United States and other industrialized nations clearly refutes Marx' contention. Since his time, the capitalist system has been characterized by a rise, not a drop, in both numbers and influence of the middle-income group, which Marx predicted would disappear.

The very fact that Communists first came to power in Russia also disproves Communist theory. According to Marx and Engels, communism would develop first in the highly industrialized countries. Russia was a predominantly agricultural country when Communists seized power in 1917. Russia was entirely unprepared for a Communist revolution by the standards which Communist theoreticians say must exist. Similarly, with the possible exceptions of Czechoslovakia and East Germany, all the other nations in the Communist bloc also were predominantly agricultural, rather than industrial, when Communists gained control of them. Thus, the Communist-bloc nations themselves show conclusively that communism has not developed from a so-called class struggle between the working class and the capitalist class.

The United States stands today as living proof of the outmoded and illogical concepts of Marxism. According to those concepts, one would expect to find that, during the past hundred years, the antagonisms between employers and workers would have intensified and erupted into a revolution which would have brought a Communist government to power. But Marxism did not foresee that the ownership of large corporations would be in the hands of thousands of stockholders. Neither did it foresee factors such as the role of labor unions in bargaining with employers for higher wages, shorter hours, and improved working conditions, along with the enactment of legislation designed to protect the owners of small businesses.

History Influenced by Many Factors

History is a far more complex process than is reflected in the oversimplified Communist interpretation. Undoubtedly, economic developments have influenced the course of history. But to say, as Communists do, that they have been the fundamental cause of all historical progress is a gross misstatement. Such an interpretation relegates the role of the individual to secondary importance in the historical process. It minimizes the effect on history of such figures as Alexander the Great, Julius Caesar, Martin Luther, William the Conquerer, Archimedes, Galileo, Copernicus, Sir Isaac Newton, George Washington, Thomas Jefferson, Abraham Lincoln, Napoleon, Madame Curie, Adolf Hitler, Benito Mussolini, Sir Winston Churchill, Albert Einstein, and even Karl Marx himself.

Communists declare that history would have been fundamentally the same whether or not these figures had ever lived. The Communist view also minimizes such motivating factors as patriotism, quest for justice, dedication to public service, pursuit of personal power, religious beliefs, love, ideals, traditions, and the search for truth, any one of which can be much more decisive than economics.

The study of history would be greatly simplified if all human activity could be traced to economic causes. But how does economics explain the Crusades? Does it explain the formation of Israel as a separate state following World War II? Does it explain the settlement of our country by refugees from religious and political persecution in Europe? Can economic determinism explain the anti-Communist uprisings in East Germany and Hungary?

The Communists have a difficult time accounting for the effect on history of natural disasters, epidemics, or even chance. History is full of incidents which seemed minor at the time but materially altered the course of events. The destruction of the great Spanish Armada, for example, was caused not only by a defeat at the hands of the English, but also by the accident of a subsequent violent storm. We are all familiar with the story of the "falling apple" and the formulation of the law of gravitation by Sir Isaac Newton. The decision by German authorities to allow Lenin to return to Russia in 1917 placed him at the scene of the revolution and had consequences far beyond those anticipated.

Despite Communist claims, the laws of natural science cannot be applied to social science. History and sociology can never be exact sciences like chemistry and physics. Scientific laws must have universal application. Historical materialism falls far short of this requirement.

As we have seen, Communists claim that, when society is no longer divided into hostile classes, the dialectic will automatically cease to operate in the area of man's social development. However, they make no effort to explain who will decide where the individual will work or what will satisfy his needs. Will each person be permitted to determine his own abilities and needs of life by the standard "from each according to his ability, to each according to his needs"? Obviously, this would lead to chaos. In any complex society, some administrative authority will have to decide the answers to these questions. But in making the decisions, there are bound to be contradictions—a clash of interests between the central authority and the citizens and even among the citizens themselves. Why will this clash not lead to class warfare and result in a sudden "leap" to another still "higher" form of society?

Communist Morality

From the concept of historical materialism with its promise of a society which will meet all the needs of man's life, Communists derive not only a "mission" to lead mankind to communism, but also a measure of values—their moral code. Communist morality is highly flexible. It is based on a single premise—anything that promotes progress toward communism is necessarily good, and anything that interferes with that progress is necessarily bad. Communists call this standard of morality "proletarian utility." Convinced that capitalism is evil, Communists say they are morally justified in using any and all means to bring about its destruction and to establish in its place a world-wide Communist society. Communists completely reject not only the traditional Judaeo-Christian concept of morality, with its objective standards of what is right and what is wrong, but also the very idea itself that there can be *any* objective standard of morality. By the standards of Communist morality, nothing is absolute, final, or sacred—except communism itself.

False Prophets

To summarize: Communists assert that, when the philosophy of materialism and the dialectical method are combined in dialectical materialism and applied to history, the result enables them to interpret the past, understand the present, and chart an inevitable future course for mankind. However, Karl Marx and Friedrich Engels proved to be false prophets. Many of their theories became outdated even during their own life spans. They did not foresee that their revolutionary theories, when put into practice by V. I. Lenin, would create a new ruling class far more powerful and ruthless in its exploitation of the workers than the factory owners of the nineteenth century.

Part Three

Power Structure

Chapter 4

The Road to Power

The Industrial Revolution ushered in an era of social, political, and economic upheaval that was to have profound effect upon the course of events in the twentieth century. The sweeping changes wrought by the Industrial Revolution had given rise to numerous reform and revolutionary movements throughout the world. Marxism was one of these movements, but its influence differed greatly in the various countries where its impact was felt. This is most clearly illustrated by the contrast between the development of Marxism in the United States and its development in Russia. *However, the unique nature and role of all Communist parties have been shaped by the Russian revolutionary tradition and Vladimir I. Lenin's organization and leadership.*

Marxism Imported to United States

The roots of present-day communism in the United States are not native to this country. The first Marxian Socialists arrived here from Germany as early as the middle of the nineteenth century. Later, during the 1870's and 1880's, additional waves of European immigrants brought with them not only the theory of Marx and Engels but also the theories of men such as Ferdinand

Lassalle (1825–1864) and Mikhail Bakunin (1814–1876), whose ideas differed, as we shall see, in marked respects from those of Marx and Engels.

One of the pioneer Marxists in this country was Joseph Weydemeyer (1818–1866), a friend of Marx and Engels. After his arrival in this country in 1851, he attempted to project their theory to other German emigres through German-language publications. Weydemeyer, who previously had been an artillery officer in the Prussian Army, enlisted in the Union Army as a captain and ultimately retired as a general. Following his military service in the Civil War, he edited a Marxist publication in St. Louis until his death in 1866.

Friedrich Sorge (1826–1906) was another pioneer in the Marxist movement here. Like Weydemeyer, Sorge was a German immigrant. He became the leading figure of a Communist club organized in New York City in 1857. Sorge, who maintained contact with Marx and Engels through correspondence, served as the leader of the American branch of the First International from 1869 until 1876. When Marx established the world headquarters of the First International in New York City in 1872, he placed Sorge in charge.

Although Marx had viewed the United States as an ideal country for the development of communism, he devoted surprisingly little attention to events here. Engels, on the other hand, offered considerable encouragement and advice to their followers and visited the United States in 1888. After Marx died, Engels wrote frequently to the handful of Marxists here indicating that he was greatly impressed with "American energy and vitality." However, Engels sharply criticized what he called a lack of theoretical development in the various Socialist movements here and said he considered the *Communist Manifesto* "far too difficult for America."

Dissension and Factionalism

Part of the problem confronting the diverse Socialist elements in this country arose from the fact that, when they came here, they brought with them the bitter controversy in which European Socialists were engaged. The principal point of contention was the basic difference between the Marxists, who stressed trade union activity to achieve economic goals, and the Lassallians, who emphasized independent political activity to accomplish their objectives. These conflicting views were responsible to a great extent for the internal dissension within the Socialist movement here from its inception and provided the basis of organization for various Socialist parties which operated in the United States prior to World War I.

Among these diverse groups was the Socialist Labor party, founded in 1877. There was also the Socialist party, which was established in 1901. Another, organized in 1905, was the Industrial Workers of the World; its members were popularly known as the "Wobblies."

Internal dissensions among the Socialists were further aggravated by personal rivalries among leaders of the various factions. Men like Eugene Debs (1855–1926), Morris Hillquit (1869–1933), Daniel DeLeon (1852–1914), and William ("Big Bill") Haywood (1869–1928) were attempting to organize the Socialist movement in this country according to their individual viewpoints.

Despite internal dissension among its advocates, the Socialist movement made some progress in the United States. It reached the peak of its influence politically in 1912 when more than 1,000 Socialists held elective public office, largely at the municipal level. In addition, its advocates were publishing eight foreign-language and five English-language daily newspapers, as well as 262 English-language and 36 foreign-language weekly periodicals. However, the Socialists still represented a protest movement, rather than a major political force in this country.

Diverse Impact of Marxism

Meanwhile, a number of notable social, economic, and political changes were occurring on the American scene. The workers in the United States were making progress not, as Marx and Engels had anticipated and predicted, by overthrowing the capitalist system, but rather by working for legitimate reforms within the system. A Department of Labor was established by the federal government in 1913. The Clayton Act of 1914 curbed the use of injunctions against the labor movement by federal courts. Many states adopted such measures as minimum wage laws, industrial safety regulations, and workmen's compensation benefits for employees injured on the job. The resiliency of the American democratic system in achieving these and similar reforms blunted the impact of Socialist, and particularly Marxist, views in this country.

Marxism pursued different courses in other countries. The direction it took in Russia was to have a profound impact on the subsequent history of practically every nation, because it was there that the theories of Marx and Engels were developed into communism as we know it today. Modern communism owes many of its basic characteristics to the fact that it first came to power in Russia—a nation that was not only industrially backward but also either unable or unwilling to adapt itself to meet the changing social, economic, and political needs of its people as our own country and the enlightened nations of Western Europe did.

Early Russian Revolutionaries

Russia did not begin its transition from the medieval to the modern era until the reign of Peter the Great (1682–1725), and its progress was slow. Despite its territorial expansion and increased importance as a European power under subsequent rulers, Russia, as late as the nineteenth century, remained an autocracy with an agricultural economy based on serfdom. The serfs—the largest class in Russia—remained virtual slaves. The cruelty with which they were treated and the wretched conditions under which they lived led to a number of uprisings, some of which reached sizable proportions.

What historians regard as the true Russian revolutionary tradition began during the Napoleonic Wars (1803–1815). Russian military officers had been exposed to the ideals of liberty and equality associated with the French Revolution. In turn, they influenced a small group of Russian intellectuals, and secret study and discussion groups were organized in opposition to the czar. Although unsuccessful, an uprising in December, 1825, by a small group of military officers, thereafter known as the Decembrists, marked the emergence of the actual revolutionary movement in Russia.

For the most part, the early Russian revolutionaries were utopian Socialists influenced by French Socialist thought. Their political protests against the czarist regime were closely related to their opposition against not only serfdom but also capitalism, symbolized by the merchants who were appearing in increasing numbers as a result of the development of commerce and industry.

Grudging reforms made by the czarist rulers failed to satisfy either the serfs or the revolutionaries. The former continued to engage in sporadic rioting, and the latter continued to plot the downfall of the czarist regime.

The radical intelligentsia saw in the still-discontented serfs a mass base of support for their own revolutionary aims. They adopted the slogan *Vnarod* (To the People) and became known as *Narodniki* (Populists). They were convinced that common ownership of the land among the Russian peasantry could serve as the basis for a unique type of socialism based on the peasants, rather than the industrial workers. Thus, to the Russian peasantry, they assigned the revolutionary role Karl Marx had given to industrial workers.

The Populists were influenced by a wide range of views. They included those of such violent revolutionaries as Mikhail Bakunin, Sergei Nechaev (1847–1882), and Peter Tkachev (1844–1885), all of whom stressed the role of a conspiratorial, revolutionary, minority group which would lead the revolution in a forcible seizure of power. But other views were expressed by men like Alexander Herzen (1812–1870) and Peter Lavrov (1823–1900), who bitterly opposed the concept of a conspiratorial minority imposing its revolution upon the people.

The status of a revolutionary in Russia during the last half of the nineteenth century was a particularly perilous and unstable one. On the one hand, the sporadic clashes with czarist forces usually resulted in defeat followed by execution or imprisonment. Those who escaped clashed among themselves over the issue of the use of terrorism as the means to the end. The dissolution of one group would inevitably result in the organization of another, or even several, depending upon the reason for the dissolution of the first.

The Populists, for example, were being arrested by the hundreds. In 1876, those still at large reorganized under the name *Zemyla i Volya* (Land and Liberty). But, within three years, this organization split over the question of the use of terrorism. The majority, which favored such tactics, formed another organization, *Narodnaya Volya* (People's Will). Its members believed that only by assassination of the leading figures of the czarist regime could they succeed in their aims. In 1881, it did succeed in assassinating Czar Alexander II, but no popular uprising occurred. A new and more severe wave of repression followed.

In 1887, a plot to assassinate the succeeding czar, Alexander III, was detected. Five conspirators were apprehended and executed. One of them was Alexander Ilyich Ulyanov, whose younger brother, Vladimir Ilyich Ulyanov, was to achieve world renown in the twentieth century under the pseudonym of V. I. Lenin.

Russian Marxists

The leaders of the minority faction of Land and Liberty, who had opposed the use of terrorism, fled to Western Europe. The group included George Plekhanov (1857–1918), generally conceded to be the father of the Russian Marxist movement; Paul Alcxrod (1850–1928); and Vera Zasulich (1851–1919). This group became convinced that socialism would be achieved in Russia only when the radical intelligentsia had gained the support of the emerging working class, rather than the peasants as the Populists believed.

Plekhanov's followers formed the Group for the Emancipation of Labor in 1883. Their purpose was to propagandize their views in Russia, where secret study classes were being formed. In 1895, Lenin was arrested as a result of his activities in one of these study groups.

The role which Vladimir I. Lenin (1870–1924) was to play in the development of modern communism was to disprove effectively another Communist theory—the theory which relegates the individual to a secondary role in the course of historical development. This one man, practically alone, transformed communism from an abstract theory into a revolutionary movement and profoundly altered the course of history.

Lenin—the Young Revolutionary

Like Karl Marx, Lenin came from a respectable family. His father had worked his way up to the position of nobleman-bureaucrat through his job as inspector of schools at Simbirsk (now known as Ulyanovsk), where Lenin was born on April 10, 1870.

When Lenin was 15 years of age, his father died. He had barely recovered from this shock when his older brother, Alexander, was executed the following year for his implication in the plot to assassinate the czar. Years later, Lenin revealed that when he was 16 years of age, he stopped believing in God.

Although he was a good student, Lenin's career in school was a stormy one. In the fall of 1887, he entered the University of Kazan to study law, but was expelled in December of the same year because of his participation in a student protest demonstration. He lived under police supervision at the family estate in Kukushkino until the fall of 1888, when he was permitted to return to Kazan but denied permission to re-enter the university. It was here that Lenin began to study the writings of Marx, who had died when Lenin was only 12.

Conspiratorial Techniques

In 1890, Lenin was granted permission to take the law examination. After a year of intense study, he took it and passed. In 1892, he began to practice law in Samara (now known as Kuibyshev), but was never a successful attorney, probably because he devoted most of his time to a secret Marxist discussion group. Also living in Samara were a number of former members of People's Will who had completed terms of imprisonment or exile. From them, Lenin learned about conspiratorial techniques—underground printing presses, fraudulent passports, codes, invisible inks—which had been developed to evade the czarist police.

Lenin became convinced that the emerging working class was destined to become the revolutionary force in Russia. In 1893, he moved to St. Petersburg, where he devoted much of his time to Marxist discussion groups and concentrated on launching attacks against the agrarian Socialist views of the Populists.

The czarist secret police thought they could use the activities of the Marxists as a wedge to split the Russian revolutionary movement. They relaxed their censorship and permitted the publication of Marxist works provided that they were written in an academic or scientific vein and were not inflammatory. Lenin and the other Marxists expounded their revolutionary views in veiled phraseology, often referred to as Aesopian language—after the fables of Aesop. As Lenin described this technique, ". . . the theory of revolutionary Marxism suddenly forces its way into the *censored* literature, written in Aesopian language, but understood by the 'interested.' "

Books became increasingly important to Lenin. He used them, not only to formulate ideas, but also to transmit secret messages. After a siege of pneumonia in 1895, he was granted permission to go abroad. He used the opportunity to visit Switzerland and contacted Plekhanov and Axelrod of the Group for the Emancipation of Labor. They discussed means of smuggling books and periodicals into Russia. On his return to St. Petersburg, Lenin carried with him a supply of prohibited books hidden in a false-bottomed suitcase. But he had not escaped the notice of the secret police. After following him for several weeks, they arrested him, in December, 1895, just as he was preparing to publish an underground newspaper.

Despite the setback, books remained important to Lenin. He served 14 months in jail in St. Petersburg and then spent almost three years in exile in Siberia. However, during the period of his imprisonment and exile, he received and returned numerous bundles of books which he used in preparing his own books and articles. Somewhere in each packet—hidden in the binding, written in invisible ink, or indicated by special markings in the text—were secret messages. Thus, he was able to maintain contact with revolutionary circles in Russia, with the political exiles in Western Europe, and with other revolutionaries in Siberia. Before long, Lenin had become the recognized leader of Marxists in Siberia.

During Lenin's exile, a significant development occurred in the Marxist movement in Russia. In 1897, the Bund was organized secretly. It was significant because its members were predominantly factory workers unlike the earlier Marxist groups which were composed, for the most part, of the radical intelligentsia. Representatives of the Bund met in 1898 with representatives of the Group for the Emancipation of Labor and founded the Russian Social Democratic Labor party. Eventually, this became the Communist Party of the Soviet Union.

A New Type of Party

Meanwhile, in Siberia, Lenin's plans for the future were taking shape. His extensive study of Marxism, of the conflicting interpretations of Marx' views, and of developments within Russia had given him definite ideas regarding the future tactics to be employed in the revolutionary movement in Russia. Occupying an important part of his thinking were the concepts of his predecessors, Bakunin, Nechaev, and Tkachev, concerning the role of a conspiratorial, revolutionary minority group which would lead the revolution in a forcible seizure of power.

Lenin's plans, which he later set forth in the book *What Is To Be Done?*, published in 1902, were to have world-wide implications. His basic concept was that the working class if left to its own devices would develop what he termed "only trade union consciousness." By this he meant that, if the working class could achieve social, economic, and political gains under capitalism, as had been the case in Western Europe during the last half of the nineteenth century, it would be content with these mere reforms and would not recognize the necessity for overthrowing the capitalist system.

Lenin's second basic principle flowed from the first. Since the workers, of themselves, lacked the necessary "political consciousness," they must be indoctrinated and led by a group possessing it. This group, as Lenin visualized it, would furnish the necessary political leadership and direction for the working class to play its role successfully in a revolution. The members of this elite group, versed in Communist theory, would serve as the vanguard. When conditions were ripe, the elite group would give the signal and lead the working class to victory in overthrowing the capitalist society.

Professional Revolutionaries

Lenin conceived of his vanguard group as a highly centralized, flexible, disciplined, and militant organization of "professional revolutionaries." He realized that, under the strict control imposed on political activity in Russia, an orthodox political party could never supplant the czarist regime. Professional revolutionaries who would devote not their spare time but, in Lenin's words, "the whole of their lives" to the cause were the answer.

Lenin established rigid standards for his proposed organization. Its members must be prepared to make any personal sacrifice and adopt any and all tactics to achieve their goal. Rather than a large, loosely organized group, the organization must be "a small, compact core, consisting of reliable, experienced and hardened workers . . . absolutely devoted and loyal to the revolution."

The inherent conspiratorial nature of Lenin's vanguard organization is indicated by his insistence that:

> . . . We must . . . exert all our efforts to devise methods of greater secrecy in our work, to conduct systematic propaganda explaining the proper methods of conducting the work, proper methods of deceiving the gendarmes and of avoiding the snares of the police. . . .

Democratic Centralism

Essential to the development and operation of the highly centralized and disciplined group which Lenin envisioned was the means of firm control. Lenin's concept, known as democratic centralism, solved the problem. Theoretically, it is designed to promote widespread discussion by all party members before party policy is adopted. Once a decision has been reached on a matter of policy, it becomes binding on all members of the party.

In actual practice, democratic centralism has provided the means by which party leaders have been able to keep a firm hand on the reins of party activities. Since Lenin's time, decisions in Communist parties have been made by the top party leaders with only limited, channeled, and largely meaningless discussion permitted in certain instances. Prior to a party congress or convention, for example, the party leaders present a proposed program for "discussion" by the membership. Few, if any, proposals are submitted by the membership at the convention, which merely rubber-stamps the program of the leadership and makes it binding on all members.

Organizing the Party

Lenin had also worked out the means by which his uniquely different type of political party would be organized. The key was to be the publication abroad of an all-Russian newspaper which would be smuggled into Russia and distributed by a network of secret agents. Lenin was confident that the paper would become the unifying force of the entire Russian revolutionary movement, providing it with both theoretical and practical guidance. Thus, the newspaper would serve, as Lenin saw it, not only as a vehicle for propaganda and agitation but also as a valuable organizational tool.

The editors of the paper—Lenin of course was to be one—would be the recognized leaders of the party. A network of secret agents distributing it would be the "skeleton of the organization." Lenin selected the paper's name *Iskra* (The Spark), and its motto, "Out of the spark shall spring the flame."

Lenin's exile in Siberia ended in 1900, and he immediately went into action. After a brief visit to Russia, he went to Switzerland for discussions with Plekhanov and Axelrod about the publication of *Iskra*. Arrangements were made for its printing in Germany, and the first issue made its appearance in December, 1900. Copies were folded into small packets, sent to professional smugglers on the Russian border, and turned over to Lenin's agents in Russia. Gradually, other covert distribution channels into Russia were developed through various cities in Sweden, France, Egypt, and Persia.

In Russia, Lenin's agents faithfully carried out their assigned tasks. When issues of *Iskra* were received by them, they produced additional copies on secret printing presses which they had managed to set up for the purpose. Then, at considerable personal risk, they passed them on to other agents or left them during the night on the streets or at factory gates to be found by the workers in the morning.

From abroad, Lenin maintained close contact with his *Iskra* agents in Russia. He corresponded extensively with them either personally or through his wife, Nadezhda Krupskaya, whom he had installed as secretary of *Iskra*. Gradually, Lenin's vision of a corps of trained revolutionaries began to take shape—a corps which he was slowly transforming into an almost separate and distinct organization loyal to him alone.

Bolsheviks and Mensheviks

Lenin's dream that *Iskra* would become the unifying force of the Russian revolutionary movement was doomed to failure. There were widespread disagreements regarding theory and tactics among the Russian Marxists, both in Russia and abroad. It also developed that Lenin's view of unification, like Marx', in effect meant complete capitulation to his will.

In an effort to unite the opposing factions, representatives of the Russian Social Democratic Labor party held a unification congress in 1903. It lasted 37 turbulent sessions, the first 13 in Brussels and the remainder in London. Lenin's careful organizational preparations for the congress were designed to give him a clear majority of the delegates.

A major dispute arose at the congress regarding the qualifications for party membership. The dispute arose over a seemingly insignificant difference in wording between a proposal submitted by Lenin defining the qualifications and an alternate proposal defining them. Lenin's proposal was designed to restrict membership to disciplined revolutionaries working actively under party direction. He argued that the alternate proposal would open membership to anyone agreeing with the party program and willing to work occasionally in support of it, but not necessarily subject to party discipline.

The struggle Lenin waged over this apparently minor point illustrates his thoroughness of planning. His plans for the formation of a narrow party of trained revolutionaries had been drawn too precisely for him to tolerate the possibility of the formation of a broad, mass party whose members would have a voice in determining party policy. This would have been possible under the alternate proposal.

On the decisive ballot regarding the qualifications for party membership, Lenin lost by a close vote. But Lenin was not easily defeated. He succeeded in forcing through several resolutions which caused several blocs of delegates to walk out in protest. Lenin emerged with a contrived majority and immediately adopted the name Bolsheviks (from the Russian word for majority) for his faction. The minority faction came to be known as Mensheviks. In succeeding years, Lenin was to retain the Bolshevik label, even though his view frequently was a minority one and even though, on occasion, he found himself standing alone.

Vanguard Role

Thus, Lenin created a unique type of political organization—one guided solely by the goal of attaining power, regardless of the methods employed or the hardships endured. His group of highly trained professional revolutionaries was to develop, through the

Bolsheviks, into the Communist Party of the Soviet Union and, by extension, into every other Communist party throughout the world. Although the organizational principles established by Lenin were designed to create a party which could operate under the repressive political conditions in Russia at a time when it was still predominantly an agricultural country, these same organizational principles still govern the parties which comprise the international Communist movement today.

Today, all Communist parties still portray themselves as elite leadership groups. They still claim to be playing a vanguard role in providing political leadership for the workers of the particular country in which they are operating. Each and every one of them is still bound by the principle of democratic centralism to insure party discipline. And, like *Iskra,* Communist publications continue to be used not only as propaganda and agitation organs but also as collective organizers—focal points for additional party activity. Today, every Communist party is striving constantly to develop its corps of professional revolutionaries who will answer Lenin's appeal for those willing to devote "the whole of their lives" to the cause of communism.

Chapter 5

The Seizure of Power

The events of 1917 made it a momentous year in history. Americans look back on that year as the one which marked the entry of the United States into World War I. But for Communists, both in this country and abroad, the year 1917 has a different significance. To them, it is the year in which the "Great October Socialist Revolution" occurred. Through that revolution, Communists seized power in Russia.

The revolution occurred on October 25, 1917, according to the Julian calendar then in use in Russia. Hence, the term "October Revolution." Under the Gregorian calendar, which is used by the Western world and has now been adopted by the Soviets, the date is November 7, 1917.

Since 1917, Communist propaganda has consistently presented the first Communist seizure of power in terms of glowing praise. A typical tribute was made in 1957 by Soviet Premier Nikita S. Khrushchev in a statement launching the celebration of the fortieth anniversary of the revolution. He described it as an event "of the greatest importance in human history" through which the "world was shaken to its foundations."

Through the years, Communists in the United States have paid equal tribute to the so-called glorious revolution. They even have attempted through their propaganda to liken it to the American Revolution, through which this nation gained its independence. In their propaganda, they have extolled men such as Benjamin Franklin and Thomas Jefferson. They have praised the Declaration of Independence and the Constitution. Through such efforts, they have attempted to transfer the respect which Americans have for these illustrious men and historic documents to respect for the revolution in Russia in November, 1917.

Communist propagandists throughout the world have enjoyed great success in their efforts to glorify the Communist seizure of power in Russia. Despite the evidence which discloses that the Communist victory in Russia in November, 1917, resulted in the imposition of a tryanny greater even than the Russian people had experienced under the czars, millions of individuals have paid tribute to the event.

A Counterfeit Revolution

The truth is that the "Great October Socialist Revolution" was actually a counterfeit revolution. Its counterfeit nature accounts for the relentless efforts by Communist propagandists through the years to glorify it. These efforts are aimed at blurring the fact that there were two revolutions in Russia in 1917. The first, which occurred in March, 1917, resulted in overthrow of the czarist regime and establishment of the Provisional Government which has been described as the freest government Russia had ever experienced. The second, the Communist seizure of power on November 7, 1917, ended the Russian people's brief period of freedom.

The czarist government fell in March, 1917, as a result of the overwhelming discontent of the people. Support for the overthrow came from elements of the population which included workers, peasants, the armed forces, the intelligentsia, and even the nobility.

The czarist regime was replaced by the Provisional Government organized along democratic lines. However, the latter took over at a time of national chaos. Lenin exploited the weakness and indecision of the Provisional Government in coping with its problems and organized an armed seizure of power by his disciplined minority group of professional revolutionaries—the Bolsheviks.

Lenin's Bolsheviks, although a small minority, seized power in Russia in 1917 not only by the use of force, but also through superior organization and discipline, by exploiting a chaotic situation at a time when their opposition was disorganized and ineffective.

Increasing Unrest in Czarist Russia

The overthrow of the czarist regime by the Russian people in March, 1917, was the culmination of a revolutionary movement that had begun almost a century before with the Decembrists. The dawn of the twentieth century had provided no cessation of czarist repressions. In 1903, a series of strikes involving approximately 250,000 workers, protesting low wages and poor working conditions, spread throughout Russia.

The unrest subsided temporarily in 1904, when the Japanese attack on the Russian fleet at Port Arthur precipitated the Russo-Japanese War (1904–1905). However, the aroused patriotism of the people soon gave way to resentment against the czarist regime to an even greater degree when Russian troops suffered a series of military defeats in the Far East.

In July, 1904, a czarist official was assassinated. Demonstrations were held calling for freedom of speech and the press, equality for national minority groups, and the formation of a representative assembly.

In January of the following year, a demonstration was organized to petition the czar for an eight-hour day, a minimum wage, the elimination of overtime work, and other benefits. What started out as a peaceful demonstration was to end as a tragic blot on the pages of Russian history. A crowd estimated at 200,000 unarmed men, women, and children participated. But when they approached the Winter Palace in St. Petersburg, the czar's troops opened fire. The disastrous results gave the day its name—Bloody Sunday. This event caused widespread indignation against the czar and destroyed the last remaining traces of public faith in the regime.

The Revolution of 1905

Bloody Sunday marked the beginning of the 1905 revolution. A wave of strikes, peasant insurrections, military mutinies, and nationalist revolts swept the country. Within a month, the czar's uncle, the governor general of Moscow, was assassinated. In August, 1905, the czar issued a decree which included a provision for the creation of a popular assembly, the Duma, which was to be granted advisory but not legislative power.

The people were not appeased. The strikes, demonstrations, and riots continued. The net result was the great general strike of October, 1905, which extended to more than a hundred cities and in which workers of practically every industry, trade, and profession participated. Faced with this situation, the czar issued a manifesto granting certain civil rights, including freedom of speech and press, and providing that no law could be enacted without the consent of the Duma.

Lenin, unswervingly committed to the seizure of power, thought that the situation was opportune for him. As soon as he learned of Bloody Sunday, he advocated an armed uprising. From exile in Switzerland, he began purchasing arms and arranging for them to be smuggled into Russia. He also studied intensively the techniques of insurrection.

Organization of the Soviets

Lenin returned to Russia in November, 1905. By that time, the Soviet (Council) of Workers' Deputies had been organized in St. Petersburg by the Mensheviks and Socialist revolutionaries. The latter were the inheritors of the tradition of the Populists. Soon, additional soviets were organized in other cities.

The soviets were the first elected bodies representing the Russian workers. As committees directing the general strike, they quickly gained considerable power. While abroad, Lenin had been opposed to the soviets, regarding them as rivals of the Bolsheviks for the role of leader of the workers. However, after he returned to Russia he quickly realized that the soviets could be useful in helping to overthrow the czarist regime, and he immediately began advocating an expansion of their functions.

Events came to a head in December, 1905. The St. Petersburg soviet, under the leadership of Leon Trotsky, its vice chairman, called on the Russian people to overthrow the czarist government. Although Trotsky was a Marxist, he did not consider himself either a Bolshevik or a Menshevik. (However, Trotsky was later to play an important role in the Bolshevik seizure of power in

1917.) Following their appeal to the Russian workers, the leaders of the St. Petersburg soviet were arrested, and all the newspapers which had published the text of the appeal were suppressed.

Meanwhile, Lenin and his Bolshevik followers were getting ready to make their move. When another general strike broke out in Moscow on December 20, 1905, it quickly developed into an insurrection in which the Bolsheviks participated. But the up- rising was quickly suppressed and Lenin was subjected to severe criticism by some of his followers for advocating revolutionary action prematurely. Lenin defended his position, pointing out that the action had provided the Bolsheviks with invaluable train- ing and experience in revolutionary tactics.

The suppression of the Moscow insurrection and arrest of the leaders of the St. Petersburg soviet, along with the ending of the Russo-Japanese War and the promise of a Duma and a constitu- tion, all contributed toward re-establishing the strength of the czarist regime. Its strength was demonstrated when the Duma convened in May, 1906, and submitted proposals for reforms which the czar considered unacceptable. In July, he ordered the Duma dissolved and new elections held. When the second Duma proved to be even more radical in its demands, the czar also ordered its dissolution in June, 1907. The electoral laws were re- vised so that, when the next Duma convened in November of that year, the majority of its members were wealthy landowners, state officials, and other supporters of the czarist government.

In addition to turning the Duma into a servile instrument of his regime, the czar made other moves to restrict his opposition. Censorship was imposed. Many unions were banned, and union members were punished for their activity in the 1905 strikes. Those unions which were permitted to operate were kept under close police supervision. Acts of terrorism were severely punished.

Between Revolutions

From the end of the 1905 revolution to the beginning of World War I, the Russian revolutionary movement was torn by one fac- tional struggle after another. The split between the Bolsheviks and the Mensheviks never actually healed and became permanent in 1912, when Lenin read the Mensheviks out of the Russian Social Democratic Labor party at its Sixth Congress in Prague. In addition, there was factionalism within the Bolshevik and the

Menshevik groups, as well as within the Socialist Revolutionary party. These disagreements were caused by theoretical differences, divergent views regarding tactics in connection with the 1905 revolution as well as subsequent developments in Russia, and the disruptive efforts of the secret police, who were trying to keep the revolutionary movement fragmented.

A major tactical difference arose among the Marxists over the issue of the "expropriations." This was a term applied to a series of armed robberies, the proceeds of which were used to finance the revolutionary movement. At its congress in Stockholm in 1906, the Russian Social Democratic Labor party ordered its members not to participate in these robberies. Lenin, who was pressed for funds, had no intention of complying. He continued to use the loot to subsidize Bolshevik publications and to maintain his personal supporters in the larger cities in Russia. In Transcaucasia, these robberies were master-minded by Joseph Djugashvili, better known as Joseph Stalin.

Several months after one such robbery in 1907, leading Bolsheviks were arrested in Paris, Munich, and Berlin while attempting to dispose of the stolen money. Additional investigation by the German police led to the discovery of a supply of bank-note paper in Berlin which had been purchased by the Bolsheviks for counterfeiting Russian rubles. The international scandal caused by these and similar incidents led the Mensheviks—and a number of Bolsheviks—to demand an investigation. However, Lenin arranged for the investigation to be conducted by a committee he controlled. The evidence was suppressed, and the investigation was effectively nullified.

The Russian revolutionary movement reached a low point in 1910. A decline in membership and police penetration of the Bolshevik ranks were important factors in this development. At the same time, there had been a gradual relaxation of some of the restrictive measures which had been imposed as a result of the 1905 revolution. For example, workers were allowed to organize unions, provided that the unions did not engage in any political activity. Then, in 1912, the czar's troops shot down striking Siberian miners, and, when this news circulated throughout Russia, protest strikes involving over 200,000 workers broke out in the industrial cities.

In the same year, the Bolsheviks began publishing a newspaper, *Pravda* (Truth), in St. Petersburg. Because of its coverage of labor unrest, factory news, and speeches by the Socialist deputies in the Duma, *Pravda's* circulation quickly increased, as did Bolshevik influence in the trade union movement.

Abdication of the Czar

When World War I broke out in 1914, Lenin was living in Austria. Realizing the opportunities for revolutionary action resulting from the outbreak of war, Lenin coined the slogan, "Transform the present imperialist war into civil war." Under this slogan, Lenin advocated that the soldiers of all armies should turn their guns on their own officers and that the working class in each country should revolt against the so-called ruling class—to convert the war between nations into a war between classes.

By 1917, as a result of military defeats, mass desertions from the army, rising inflation, and shortages of food and fuel, Russia was in a state of almost complete anarchy. When the czar ordered the Duma dissolved, the dam finally broke, and the centuries-old, pent-up emotions of the Russian people were released. Mutinying soldiers joined a hurriedly called meeting of the workers of Petrograd (now known as Leningrad), and the Soviet of Workers' and Soldiers' Deputies was organized. It immediately issued a call for the election of a constituent assembly. Backed by the Petrograd soviet, the Duma elected a provisional committee to assume control of the government. With the situation deteriorating rapidly, the czar's military advisors warned him that, if Russia were to continue in the war, he would have to abdicate.

The Provisional Government

Faced with these developments, Czar Nicholas II attempted to abdicate in favor of his brother, Grand Duke Michael. However, a committee of the Soviet of Workers' and Soldiers' Deputies refused to recognize the continuation of the 300-year-old Romanov dynasty and persuaded Michael to waive his right to the succession pending the election of a constituent assembly which would determine the nature of the future Russian government.

A committee from the Duma and the soviet met in Petrograd and appointed the members of the new Provisional Government, headed by Prince George E. Lvov and made up largely of liberal members of the Duma. The Provisional Government quickly granted complete amnesty to all political prisoners and proclaimed freedom of speech, assembly, and the press, as well as the right of workers to strike.

The revolution of March, 1917, which brought about the end of the czarist regime, enjoyed widespread popular support. Mass support came from diverse elements of the population, even though they differed in their views as to what permanent type of government should eventually replace the czarist regime.

Bolsheviks Taken by Surprise

This March revolution caught the Bolsheviks—and all other revolutionary parties—by surprise. Trotsky and Nikolai Bukharin (1888–1938) were both in New York City when it happened. The majority of the other leading Bolsheviks were political exiles elsewhere, imprisoned in Russia, or scattered throughout Siberia. Lenin was in Switzerland. Badly in need of funds, all but abandoned by most of his former supporters, virtually unknown except to a few followers in Russia, and regarded by many other Socialists as a fanatic, Lenin was at the lowest ebb of his influence. Yet, within a year, Lenin was to rule Russia.

Once political amnesty had been granted by the Provisional Government, the Bolsheviks and other revolutionaries hurried back to Russia. Lenin returned to Petrograd in April, 1917, and, shortly after his return, wrote in *Pravda* that Russia was then "the freest country in the world." But, within a few months, Lenin was to overthrow the Provisional Government that had transformed Russia into "the freest country in the world."

Lenin immediately demanded that the war with Germany be transformed into a civil war. This demand, while designed to create the chaos Lenin desired, made the defeat of Russia in World War I a certainty. He urged that the Bolsheviks withdraw their support from the Provisional Government and, at the same time, advance the slogan, "All power to the soviets." These demands stirred considerable opposition to Lenin by both Bolsheviks and other revolutionaries. The extent of this opposition to Lenin led many to miscalculate the threat he represented.

Few governments have ever taken over under more adverse circumstances than did the Provisional Government in Russia. The Russian Army was retreating under the onslaught of the advancing Germans, and rising inflation and shortages of food and fuel were adding to the already precarious economic situation. The Provisional Government struggled desperately to prevent anarchy and to restore order. The Bolsheviks under Lenin, on the other hand, were attempting to discredit the Provisional Government by promising to distribute the land to the peasants, to increase the distribution of food, and to bring the unpopular war with Germany to an immediate end.

In the period immediately following the czar's abdication, the Bolsheviks were a minority in the Petrograd soviet. But, because of the disorganization of their opponents in that council and their superior organization and intense activity, they exerted an influence far exceeding their numerical strength. In addition, Lenin's agitational slogans—"Down with the czarist Duma!," "End the War!," and "Bread, Peace and Freedom!"—reflected the sentiment of the masses. By June 1917, the Bolsheviks had emerged as the majority group, at least in the powerful Petrograd soviet.

While popular discontent was rising as a result of continuing military defeats, the Bolsheviks participated in a protest demonstration in mid-July which led to several clashes. The Provisional Government ordered the arrest of a number of Bolshevik leaders, including Lenin. With anti-Bolshevik feeling running high, Lenin fled to Finland, and Bolshevik influence declined.

Meanwhile, the military situation was growing steadily worse. In addition, in early September, 1917, General Lavr G. Kornilov, the Russian commander-in-chief, prepared to seize the reins of power from the Provisional Government. When Kornilov's plans became known, he was dismissed by Alexander Kerensky, who had succeeded Prince Lvov as prime minister in July, 1917. Kornilov then countered by ordering his troops to march on Petrograd. Under the direction of the Petrograd soviet, communications workers refused to transmit his orders, railroad workers refused to transport his troops, and agitators persuaded his troops not to fight. Kornilov's bid for power collapsed, and he was arrested.

A critical split between the military leadership and the Provisional Government resulted from Kornilov's attempt to seize power. Kerensky was left without any reliable military force and was completely dependent on the Petrograd soviet. With the political situation steadily deteriorating and with the Bolshevik leaders who had been imprisoned in July now released, Bolshevik influence began to rise rapidly again.

The Bolshevik Revolution

From his exile in Finland, Lenin, who had been following the situation in Petrograd closely, began to bombard the Bolsheviks with repeated urgings for an armed uprising. The Bolsheviks, however, were bitterly divided over this issue and spent most of September and October discussing it. It was not until October 23, 1917, that Lenin, who had secretly returned to Petrograd, won a majority of the Bolshevik Central Committee for his proposal to stage an armed uprising.

Since Lenin was still subject to arrest, the practical job of organizing the revolution fell largely to Trotsky who, since shortly after his return to Russia in the Spring of 1917, had been working closely with Lenin. In October, 1917, Trotsky had been elected chairman of the Petrograd soviet and, later that month, head of the Military Revolutionary Committee formed by the soviet.

Early on November 7, 1917, the Military Revolutionary Committee took advantage of the confusion and helplessness of the Provisional Government by staging an armed uprising in Petrograd. The Bolsheviks seized control of the telephone, postal, and telegraph offices, as well as the state bank. The members of the Provisional Government, meeting at the Winter Palace, capitulated to an ultimatum from the Bolsheviks, who obviously had superior military forces at their disposal. The Bolshevik revolution in Petrograd was accomplished with comparatively little bloodshed.

With no effective military support, Kerensky, who had briefly tried to negotiate with the Bolsheviks, was forced to flee. The Bolsheviks in Moscow also began an insurrection and, by November 15, 1917, were in control. With the capture of Petrograd and Moscow, the Bolsheviks had grasped control of the two major cities in Russia. Lenin's professional revolutionaries had triumphed.

The Bolsheviks' success was a direct result, not only of the use of force, but also of their superior organization and discipline applied in a chaotic situation at a time when their opposition was disorganized and ineffective. These have been vital elements in the formula for subsequent Communist expansion.

The views of Alexander Kerensky on both the counterfeit nature of the Bolshevik revolution and the continued efforts of Communists to expand their totalitarian rule through similar seizures of power were expressed in an article published in this country in 1947. At the time, his views were accompanied by a warning to free people everywhere that is as applicable now as it was then. Kerensky said:

> The myth that the Communists overthrew czarism has been purposely spread to conceal their crime of having strangled the first Russian democracy. And today Communists everywhere are trying to seize power by the same cynical device: posing as 'defenders of democracy,' organizing their blows against liberty under the banners of liberty. It was not until after his victory that Lenin admitted publicly that his freedom-loving slogans had been deliberate deception.
>
> The Russian people cannot be blamed for falling into the Bolshevik trap for, at that time, the world had had no experience with modern totalitarian techniques. But there is no such excuse for the millions of workers, farmers and intellectuals in the democratic West who are offered the bait today. To them the frightful experience of my native land should serve as a grim warning.

Chapter 6

Imposition of Power

The history of the modern Communist movement is a chronicle of treachery and deceit. The pages of that history abound with examples of individual and mass terrorism, broken treaties, infiltration and subversion of non-Communist governments and organizations, full-scale and guerrilla warfare, sabotage, genocide, repression of minorities, purges, assassinations, slave-labor camps, suppression of religion, the abrogation of individual liberty, and nuclear blackmail. Such are the tactics used by Communists as part of the over-all strategy through which they ultimately hope to communize the world.

Communist strategy refers to the grand, over-all, long-range plan of constant and multiple pressures against the non-Communist world. Communist tactics, on the other hand, are the immediate decisions, measures, and action necessary to attain specific Communist objectives. Tactics are quickly altered according to changing conditions, but the broad outline of strategy and its goal remain relatively fixed. Both are based upon essentially the same principles which guide successful military operations: deception, maneuverability, the acceptance of temporary setbacks in order to regroup forces for subsequent battle, long-range planning, iron discipline, and high morale based on confidence in the inevitability of victory. *Out of his experience in organizing and leading the successful Bolshevik revolution in Russia, Lenin developed fundamental Communist strategy and tactics, the ultimate objective of which is the seizure of power.*

Strategy and Tactics

Most of the diverse tactics employed by Communists today are outlined in the writings of Lenin. Although many of his tactics were developed in and applied to a set of historical circumstances peculiar to Russia late in the nineteenth and early in the twentieth century, his success in bringing communism to power through these tactics has made them sacrosanct in the eyes of Communists. While treating theoretical questions, Lenin's writings emphasize tactics, even though he had to rationalize in many cases to justify them as practical extensions of the theory of Marx and Engels.

Lenin's writings dealing with tactics have been reprinted in millions of copies in many different languages. They still are studied today by Communists in non-Communist nations, not as abstract theoretical analyses, but rather as training manuals which outline practical action in preparation for a Communist seizure of power.

A striking feature of Communist literature dealing with strategy and tactics is its use of military terms. This naturally evolves out of the similarity between the Communist idea of class struggle and the theory of military warfare. As we have seen, Communists regard all history as a record of the struggle on a wide variety of fronts between opposing classes in society. Like military campaigns, the class struggle envisioned by Communists involves alternate periods of offense and defense and of attack and retreat. This helps explain why Communist literature is saturated with military terms, such as "mobilize the masses," "advance detachment of the proletariat," "storm the fortress of capitalism," "in the front ranks of the struggle," and "shifts in the ranks."

Many of the basic tactics developed by Lenin and still in use today flow directly from his concept of the nature, role, and organization of a Communist party. Because of its conspiratorial nature, the party is not restricted in the type or the variety of tactics it employs. For example, Communist parties not only work openly but also operate through a secret or underground apparatus. As an elite corps of "professional revolutionaries,"

Communists use many tactics which are designed to influence non-Communists in an effort to achieve mass support. This is particularly true regarding what the party describes as the working class—visualized by the party as the base and source of its power. As an organization of disciplined members, the party works through other organizations such as front groups. It issues a torrent of propaganda through its newspapers, magazines, and other publications. It is tireless in its efforts to infiltrate non-Communist organizations, particularly trade unions and other labor organizations.

However, Communists do not limit their tactics to those which spring directly from the nature and role of the party itself. Other tactics, such as guerrilla warfare, are adaptations of Lenin's basic principles to specific conditions in various nations at different times. Still others, for example, Soviet policy in the Congo during 1961, can almost be described as timely improvisations to exploit favorably developing situations.

Finally, in their efforts to gain acceptance as legitimate political organizations, Communist parties use tactics common to political groups. They form temporary coalitions to achieve mutual short-range goals. They publicize their program to create the impression that they are working in the interest of the majority of the population. They sponsor candidates for election to public office, and they attack the programs of legitimate political groups.

Power Is Fundamental

Regardless of the form they take, Communist tactics have one basic, underlying objective—the seizure of power. Lenin never lost sight of that fact. In *Toward the Seizure of Power*, for example, he wrote: "The question of power . . . is the fundamental question which determines *everything* in the development of a revolution. . . ." Certainly it was the fundamental question of the Bolsheviks' counterfeit revolution of 1917 and all that was to follow. For that reason, efforts by Communists in this country to liken the Bolshevik revolution to our American Revolution are particularly absurd. But such propaganda efforts serve a valuable purpose if they cause Americans to think seriously about the nature of both revolutions, because a penetrating analysis of both clearly exposes the true nature of modern communism as a vehicle propelled by the lust for power.

Contrast in Revolutions

Many factors comprise the difference between the Bolshevik revolution and our own earlier revolution. There are differences, for example, in the motives which inspired each and in the moral codes which governed those involved, as well as differences in such things as the number of individuals concerned, their goals, and their spiritual concepts.

The rebellion of the American colonists was motivated by the desire for liberty—freedom of political, economic, and social action. But in Russia in 1917, a new freedom had been achieved by the overthrow of the czarist regime early that year to the extent that even Lenin himself proclaimed its existence. Thereupon, Lenin and his Bolsheviks proceeded to destroy it.

Lenin's statement that the question of power is the fundamental question of every revolution contrasts sharply with what the early American colonists felt the fundamental question to be. They spelled out their feelings on this point in the Declaration of Independence when they declared that "all men are created equal" and are "endowed by their Creator with certain unalienable Rights, that among these are Life, Liberty and the pursuit of Happiness."

There is a vast difference too in the moral code that governed the men of American revolutionary times and those of Lenin's revolutionary movement. Dedicated to a noble ideal, the early American colonists pledged to support each other with their lives, fortunes, and sacred honor in quest of that ideal. But Lenin was not to be bound by any of the traditional moral, legal, or ethical restraints. To him, any action—violent or peaceful, open or covert, legal or illegal, moral or immoral—which would advance communism was automatically justified. From the claim of Marx and Engels that there are no eternal moral laws, it was but a short step to Lenin's pronouncement that "morality is entirely subordinated to the interests of the class struggle of the proletariat" and that a "morality taken outside of human society . . . is a fraud."

In contrasting the differences between the two revolutions, the basic spiritual concept of the one and the total rejection of such a concept in the other should not be overlooked. Turning again to the Declaration of Independence, we see the concept stated by our founding fathers in their expressed "firm reliance on the protection of Divine Providence." But to Marx and Lenin religion was "the opium of the people." Lenin scorned religion as a "kind of spiritual gin in which the slaves of capital drown their human shape and their claims to any decent human life."

Another important difference between the American Revolution and the Bolshevik seizure of power involves the will of the people. Communist propagandists depict the Bolshevik seizure of power as a "proletarian" revolution. In reality, it was an armed insurrection by a relatively small group against an almost powerless government. Despite Communist propaganda claims attempting to show that Lenin had the overwhelming support of the workers and peasants when he seized power, the fact is that he and his Bolshevik followers constituted a minority and continued to remain one even after the seizure.

On the other hand, the minority of American patriots responsible for sparking the revolt against British rule were joined by steadily increasing numbers of colonists who became converted to the idea of political freedom. Their success has been magnified by the contributions of millions of people in subsequent generations who have used early American ideals as a base on which to establish a system of free government truly representative of the will of its citizens.

What little support the Bolsheviks were able to muster among the people was created by their deceptive promises of "Bread, Peace, and Freedom!" All the Russians certainly wanted bread, peace, and freedom, but the majority of them did not want Bolshevism.

The greatest difference between the American and Bolshevik revolutions was in the goal of each. Dedicated as they were to the principle that freedom under God is man's destiny, our forefathers continued to work toward that end after they had achieved their independence. They labored to provide a constitutional framework of representative government within which the individuals of the newly established nation could obtain the blessings of liberty. At the same time, they charted a course for the future development of the nation in a manner that not only would preserve the inherent dignity and worth of the individual but also would provide the means for the individual to pursue his legitimate aspirations for justice, truth, and spiritual development.

The founders of this nation sought the answers to their quest in liberty under law. Their idea of justice was based on the belief that there is a rule of law above the rule of men. They dedicated themselves to this concept in the Declaration of Independence.

Those who came after them, beset though they were by the mounting difficulties of a growing nation, rededicated themselves to the same concept and continued to use it as the keystone in their development of a peaceful and bountiful society.

The Dictatorship of the Proletariat

In Russia, after the Bolshevik revolution, Lenin was not concerned with establishing a society in which individual freedom could grow and flourish. His concern was just the opposite—how to use the power he had won to advance communism, without regard for individual freedom.

"Justification" for what was ahead for the Russian people had already been worked out by Lenin prior to the revolution. During the Summer of 1917, while planning the Bolshevik seizure of power, Lenin had outlined in detail the means by which he intended to rule—through the establishment of a dictatorship of the proletariat based on naked force and terror.

In Communist theory, the term "dictatorship of the proletariat" refers to a temporary, transitional form of government between capitalism and pure communism. Communists usually describe this period as the era of socialism.

Although Marx and Engels had mentioned the dictatorship of the proletariat, neither had elaborated in any detail on its nature or duration. The most explicit statement made by Marx on the subject was his observation that:

> Between capitalist and Communist society lies the period of the revolutionary transformation of the one into the other. There corresponds to this also a political transition period in which the state can be nothing but *the revolutionary dictatorship of the proletariat.*

Lenin proceeded to build on this point skillfully and to fashion himself a vehicle to retain power. Like Marx and Engels, Lenin stressed that force and violence were essential to bring about the overthrow of capitalism. He also adhered to their views that it would be impossible to reform the capitalist state and that it was necessary to destroy it and replace it with a new political order— the dictatorship of the proletariat. This new state would have the alleged role of leading the masses toward a society of pure communism—a society of common ownership of the means of production. But in the meantime, continuing opposition could be expected from the remaining adherents of the old capitalist state. Therefore, Lenin stressed that the new state—the dictatorship of the proletariat—must have a power unrestricted by laws, both to crush existing opposition and to permit it to play its leading role for the benefit of the masses.

Lenin had previously written extensively on the need for force and violence to achieve the overthrow of capitalism. His views on the point were succinctly presented in 1917, when he declared that "The seizure of power is a matter of insurrection; its political purpose will be clear after the seizure."

Lenin was as forceful as Marx in his insistence that the Communists could not take over and reform the old political system, which had to be completely destroyed and replaced:

> The proletarian revolution is impossible without the forcible destruction of the bourgeois state machine and the substitution for it of a *new one*. . . .

The expressed reliance upon force is again shown in Lenin's observation concerning the resulting establishment of the new political order—the dictatorship of the proletariat—which would have power shared by none and would rely "directly upon the armed force of the masses."

Force and violence continued to play a prominent part in the scheme of things. Lenin warned that the remaining adherents of the old system would attempt to disrupt the efforts of the new political order to lead the masses to pure communism:

> The proletariat needs state power, the centralised organisation of force, the organisation of violence, for the purpose of crushing the resistance of the exploiters and for the purpose of *leading* the great mass of the population . . . in the work of organising socialist economy.

The formula for total power, unrestricted by law, was neatly summarized by Lenin in the statement that:

> The revolutionary dictatorship of the proletariat is power won and maintained by the violence of the proletariat against the bourgeoisie, power that is unrestricted by any laws.

Lenin's reliance on force and violence and his total rejection of any laws through which the power of the government would be restricted become even more meaningful when contrasted with the beliefs expressed in the Declaration of Independence by the founders of this nation. It will be recalled that our forefathers declared that governments are created among men for the purpose of enabling them to secure their unalienable rights. On this particular point, our forefathers stressed that governments thus created derive "their just powers from the consent of the governed."

Obviously, the dictatorship of the proletariat as developed by the Bolsheviks is an instrument of oppression. Communists themselves recognize it as such. However, they attempt to justify it with the explanation that it is an instrument of oppression by the majority over the minority as contrasted to all other state forms which they describe as instruments of oppression by the exploiting minority over the oppressed majority.

Added to this is the Communist explanation that the dictatorship of the proletariat will exist only until the pure stage of communism has been reached. However, Communist theory is extremely vague and conflicting regarding the duration of such a dictatorship. Marx and Engels saw the proletarian revolution as a spontaneous, explosive event and viewed the dictatorship of the proletariat as a transitional phase which would terminate in the not too distant future. Lenin, on the other hand, viewed the proletarian revolution as encompassing pre-revolutionary activity, the violent overthrow of the capitalist state, and the establishment and subsequent operation of the dictatorship of the proletariat for an indefinite period.

The lack of a specific prediction regarding the duration of the dictatorship of the proletariat is still characteristic of Communist theory. The Twenty-second Congress of the Communist Party of the Soviet Union, which met in Moscow in October, 1961, approved a program which, among other things, dealt with the problem. Concerning the withering away of the dictatorship of the proletariat which allegedly will occur, the program asserted with typical propaganda overtones that the Soviet Union has "built socialism" and is now in the process of establishing a Communist society. The program claimed that the dictatorship of the proletariat in the Soviet Union "has fulfilled its historic mission and has ceased to be indispensable in the U.S.S.R. from the point of view of the tasks of internal development."

In actual practice, the direction of internal affairs in the Soviet Union is still highly centralized. It makes little difference whether the directing force is called the dictatorship of the proletariat, the Communist Party of the Soviet Union, or simply the Soviet state. Moreover, the Twenty-second Congress reaffirmed the absolute necessity of retaining the state, when it declared that the "state as an organisation of the entire people will survive until the complete victory of communism." In other words, the state will not even begin to wither away until communism has triumphed on a world-wide scale.

In practical application, the theory of the dictatorship of the proletariat has resulted in the dictatorship of the Communist party. As early as 1926, Joseph Stalin was forced to admit that:

> . . . the dictatorship of the proletariat is *in essence* the 'dictatorship' of its vanguard, the 'dictatorship' of its Party, as the main guiding force of the proletariat. . . .

It is particularly significant that the Twenty-second Congress in Moscow proclaimed that the Communist party would play an even greater role in the future "as the leading and guiding force of Soviet society." In effect, the Twenty-second Congress reasserted that the Communist party has no intention of giving up the power it seized in 1917—power which it has wielded since that time without any restraint.

Reign of Terror

It is only necessary to recount a few of the events of the early days of Bolshevik rule over Russia to see how effectively Lenin wielded power—a power based on brute force and justified by him through the theoretical concept of the dictatorship of the proletariat.

A few days after the seizure of power, the Bolsheviks issued a decree restricting the publication of opposition newspapers. This soon was followed by a series of decrees outlawing other political groups. Then, in December, 1917, Lenin ordered the formation of a secret-police organization, the Cheka (Extraordinary Commission for Combating Counterrevolution and Sabotage). It was given the assignment of crushing all opposition to the Bolsheviks and was under the Council of People's Commissars (Sovnarkom), of which Lenin was chairman.

The Cheka quickly became a symbol of terror for the Russian people. The all-embracing nature of its functions and the lack of any specific restraints on its powers immediately led it to assume the powers of arrest, imprisonment, and execution with the almost automatic approval of the Sovnarkom. By February, 1918, for example, the Cheka had acquired power to shoot "counterrevolutionary agitators" on the spot. Following an unsuccessful attempt on Lenin's life and the assassination of the head of the Petrograd Cheka in August, 1918, it rounded up scores of non-Communists and summarily executed them.

Within a few months after the Bolshevik seizure of power, Lenin's tactics of violence had taken a fearful toll. The freedom of the press and the freedom of speech which had existed under the Provisional Government and which were centuries-old goals of the true Russian revolutionary tradition had been eliminated.

Brest-Litovsk

This was a period of time in which Lenin's strategy and tactical maneuvers were put to a severe test to meet both the internal and external problems confronting the Bolshevik rule. Lenin knew that to consolidate the power he had won he must end Russia's participation in World War I. On November 8, 1917, he published a peace decree calling for an immediate end to hostilities. The Bolsheviks urged Russian soldiers to fraternize with the enemy, the German Army. Military revolts against Russian generals who favored continuing the war completed the demoralization of the Russian Army, and, on November 27, 1917, Germany announced that it was prepared to begin negotiations with the Bolsheviks.

Lenin was gambling boldly. The treaty of Brest-Litovsk, which ended Russia's participation in the war, was finally signed on March 3, 1918, at Lenin's insistence and over the opposition even of many Bolsheviks who were unaware of the nature of the game Lenin was playing. Opposition to the treaty arose from the fact that Lenin, as the price paid for ending the war, was forced to cede extensive territory to Germany. But Lenin explained that he was trading space for time and that he had no intention of honoring the treaty if it could possibly be avoided.

Lenin's gamble worked. By the end of the year, under the conditions established at the conclusion of World War I, Germany was required to return to Russia the territory ceded by Lenin at Brest-Litovsk.

Lenin's admission that the treaty of Brest-Litovsk was signed as a tactical measure set a pattern which Communists have followed consistently through the years. In 1955, for example, a committee of the United States Senate published the results of a study that had been made of nearly 1,000 treaties and agreements that had been entered into by the Soviet Union. The study revealed that in a period of 38 years the Communist government of the Soviet Union had broken its word to virtually every country with which it had entered into an agreement. It was clear from this study that the Communists live up to international agreements only when it is obviously to their advantage.

Bolsheviks Repudiated

On a par with Communist tactical maneuvers in regard to treaties are their tactical maneuvers regarding elections. In the very first election held by the Bolshevik regime after its seizure of power in Russia, for example, the Communists were overwhelmingly defeated. But electoral defeat had no effect on their determination to retain power.

The demand for the election of a constituent assembly had been one of the main planks in the program of Russian revolutionary parties as early as 1905. When the czar abdicated in March, 1917, one of the primary objectives of the Provisional Government which replaced the czarist regime was to convene a constituent assembly. The Bolsheviks were no less insistent than other political groups in their demands that the Provisional Government hold such an election.

The difficulties inherent in attempting to hold a nationwide election in a country as large as Russia in 1917 constituted a massive problem. Complicating the problem was the confusion created by the overthrow of the czarist regime and its replacement by the Provisional Government. The unsettled conditions had forced the Provisional Government to delay its plans for the election on several occasions. Finally, the election was scheduled to be held on November 25, 1917.

Thus, the much-desired election was already scheduled when the Bolshevik seizure of power occurred on November 7, 1917. Since the Bolsheviks had issued strong protests each time the Provisional Government had been forced to postpone the previously scheduled elections, they felt obliged to hold it as scheduled, despite the fact that they had reason to be apprehensive of the results.

The election took place, therefore, under Bolshevik rule on November 25–27, 1917. The Bolsheviks were soundly defeated. They received only about 25 per cent of the vote and elected only 175 of the more than 700 deputies. They had been overwhelmingly repudiated by the Russian people.

Lenin's plans for the establishment of a dictatorship had been too carefully drawn for him to permit the will of the people to stand between him and his goal. The first meeting of the newly elected Constituent Assembly was scheduled to take place on January 18, 1918. Lenin and his Bolshevik followers were ready when the day arrived.

Abolishment of the Constituent Assembly

Lenin's first move was to pack the hall with heavily armed soldiers and sailors awaiting instructions from him. As soon as the meeting opened, the Bolshevik deputies began pounding their desks. They constantly interrupted other speakers. Appeals for order only gave rise to greater disruptive tactics. When the deputies of other parties tried to speak out, they were threatened by the soldiers and sailors, who aimed rifles and pistols at them.

Despite harassment by the Bolsheviks, the Constituent Assembly rejected the Bolshevik platform. The Bolshevik deputies walked out of the meeting. The next session of the assembly was scheduled to take place on the following day. But Lenin had seen enough to convince him that more forceful action was necessary. When the deputies arrived at the hall the next day, they were met by a detachment of armed troops loyal to Lenin. At the same time, the Bolsheviks issued a decree abolishing the Constituent Assembly. Thus ended the only freely elected government of the Russian people. Its first meeting had been its last.

Civil War in Russia

The Russian people did not submit meekly to the Bolshevik seizure of power. By the summer of 1918, military resistance to the rule of the Bolsheviks had flared into open civil war which continued on a widespread scale until 1920.

The eventual victory of the Bolsheviks in the civil war was due largely to Leon Trotsky. After the Provisional Government had replaced the czarist regime and declared an amnesty for political exiles, Trotsky had left his job as a journalist in New York City and had returned to Russia. Following his return, he linked forces with the Bolsheviks in July, 1917. In October of that year, he was elected chairman of the Petrograd soviet. When Lenin went into hiding during the period immediately preceding the Bolshevik revolution, Trotsky became the on-the-scene organizer of the actual insurrection. After the revolution, Trotsky held the positions of commissar of foreign affairs and commissar of war.

As commissar of war, Trotsky reorganized and revitalized the Red Army. During the period the reorganization was taking place, Finland, Lithuania, Latvia, and Estonia had proclaimed their independence from Russia and succeeded in resisting Russian efforts to reimpose control over their areas. However, efforts by the Ukrainian, Georgian, Armenian, and Azerbaijanian nationalities to establish independent states were ruthlessly suppressed despite Bolshevik pledges to grant self-determination to national minority groups.

By the spring of 1921, the Soviet Union under Communist rule was rapidly approaching economic collapse. The devastation of World War I, the civil war, the nationalization of industry by the Bolsheviks, and the refusal of the peasants to produce more crops than they needed for their own use in protest against the Communist practice of requisitioning grain all served to contribute to the chaotic economic situation.

The Kronstadt Revolt

The Communist hold on the country was put to a test in 1921 by sailors stationed at the naval fortress of Kronstadt. It was ironic that many of these same sailors had played a vital role in Lenin's successful seizure of power in 1917. At mass meetings attended by thousands of them, resolutions were passed demanding new elections by secret ballot, as well as the restoration of the freedoms of speech, press, and assembly.

Efforts by the Communists to pacify the sailors failed. The latter formed a revolutionary committee. Trotsky immediately demanded that the rebels surrender. When they refused, Communist troops and members of the Cheka crossed the ice and assaulted the island fortress. The rebellion was crushed after fierce fighting in which thousands of rebels were killed. The majority of those who were captured were executed by the Cheka, and the remainder were imprisoned.

The New Economic Policy (NEP)

The economic problems and the growing unrest, including some differences of opinion within the Communist party itself, resulted in a form of tactical retreat by Lenin. The party's Tenth Congress, which met while the Kronstadt revolt was occurring, approved elimination of the practice of requisitioning grain from the peasants and authorized a limited return to private enterprise. This marked the beginning of what is generally referred to as the New Economic Policy (NEP). As a result of the limited economic reforms that occurred under the NEP, there was a partial economic recovery in Russia toward the end of 1921. But Bolshevik agricultural policies finally led to a famine which took approximately 5,000,000 lives during 1921 and 1922.

Although Lenin had been forced to grant some economic concessions, he had no intention of relaxing discipline within the Communist party. More important to Lenin than the NEP policies adopted by the Tenth Congress were two political resolutions adopted at his insistence. One of these condemned the view of party members who contended that industry should be controlled by trade unions, an issue which was a cause of some of the differences within the party. The second resolution called for the dissolution of all such dissident groups under penalty of expulsion from the party and granted the central committee full disciplinary power. With these resolutions adopted, Lenin had strengthened the discipline of the Communist party—the root of his dictatorial power.

When Lenin died on January 21, 1924, his dictatorship of the proletariat wielded absolute power. All political opposition had been ruthlessly suppressed. Strict censorship was enforced over all means of communication. The trade unions had been transformed into adjuncts of the state. The dreaded Cheka was firmly established as an integral part of the Communist regime. Even though Lenin was dead, Marxism-Leninism, the merger of his practical action with the theory of Marx and Engels, still lived to guide the world Communist movement.

Communism Is an Ideology

The Communists have always claimed that communism is a philosophy. A philosophy is a system of thought which attempts to furnish the ultimate answer to the reason for man's existence and man's relationship to this existence. By definition, it seeks ultimate truth. For this reason, every philosophy must continually question all premises, conclusions, judgments, values, and principles. However, the validity of the basic theoretical premises of communism cannot be questioned by its adherents. These basic premises must be accepted as facts.

Communism does not permit an objective search for truth. Communism tolerates only efforts to justify the validity of its allegedly "scientific" principles. Therefore, communism is not, and cannot be, a philosophy in the strict sense of the word. It is, rather, an ideology—an interpretation of nature, history, and society which is developed with some logic from premises which are demonstrably false but which are not open to question or criticism by its adherents.

As developed by Lenin, the primary goal of this ideology is the seizure of total power by any and all means in all areas of society and on a world-wide scale by an elite minority group—the Communist party.

In light of what we have learned, we are now in a better position to understand the definition of communism which appeared in Chapter 2: *Communism (Marxism-Leninism) is the revolutionary, materialistic ideology used by its adherents to justify their efforts to seize power by any and all means for the forcible establishment of a world-wide totalitarian social order.*

People throughout the world today look back with horror on the events surrounding the Bolshevik seizure and consolidation of power in Russia. The ruthless brutality displayed by the Communists then and since that time in similar conquests in other countries gives ample evidence of their wholehearted support of the creed of force and violence developed by Lenin.

It seems particularly fitting to mention that the year 1917, which gave birth in a practical sense to Lenin's creed of violence, also gave rise to a definition of Americanism which is known as "The American's Creed." It was written by William Tyler Page, a descendant of one of the signers of the Declaration of Independence, and was later accepted by the United States House of Representatives on behalf of the American people. Those who attempt to liken the Bolshevik revolution to the American Revolution need only refer to this creed and contrast it with the history of Communist treachery to see how hypocritical their efforts are.

The American's Creed

I believe in the United States of America as a Government of the people, by the people, for the people, whose just powers are derived from the consent of the governed; a democracy in a Republic; a sovereign Nation of many sovereign States; a perfect Union, one and inseparable; established upon those principles of freedom, equality, justice, and humanity for which American patriots sacrificed their lives and fortunes.

I therefore believe it is my duty to my country to love it, to support its Constitution, to obey its laws, to respect its flag, and to defend it against all enemies.

Chapter 7

Consolidation of Power

Terror and lies are trademarks of Communist tryanny. In 1956, this fact was brought to the attention of the entire world in several shocking ways. The terror associated with Communist rule was revealed in June of that year, when a workers' demonstration against the Communist regime was crushed by tanks in Poznan, Poland. It was repeated in an even more brutal form in October of that year, when Soviet troops and tanks were used in a ruthless manner to smash the efforts of freedom-loving Hungarians to rid themselves of the oppressions of the Soviet-dominated regime.

The lies associated with the rule of Communist tyrants also were exposed for public examination in June, 1956. That was when the United States government released to newspapers information which it had obtained about the contents of a "secret speech" made in February of that year by Soviet Premier Nikita S. Khrushchev at a closed session of the Twentieth Congress of the Communist Party of the Soviet Union. In that speech, Khrushchev revealed how lies had been used to cover up the intolerance, brutality, and abuses of power that marked the tyrannical rule of Joseph Stalin during his more than 20 years of dictatorship in the Soviet Union.

In condemning Stalin's dictatorship, Khrushchev denounced

the "cult of the personality" through which Stalin had been worshipped as a hero. But Khrushchev's speech was far more than a denunciation of Stalin. It was also, in effect, an indictment of the system which, through its inherent reliance on terror and oppression, breeds such despots.

It has been shown how, in practical application, the dictatorship of the proletariat actually means the dictatorship of the Communist party. This chapter will show how the dictatorship of the Communist party results in the dictatorship of one person.

Under communism, there is no real provision for the orderly transfer of the reins of government. This is as true today as it was at the time of Lenin's death in 1924. His death precipitated a crisis—the chronic problem of all dictatorships, even the dictatorship of the proletariat—the struggle among his heirs for the vacant throne.

It was to be a ruthless struggle, featuring terror, force, and violence. Lenin had used such tactics to impose the dictatorship of the proletariat on the Russian people. His successor, Stalin, was to use them in consolidating the hold of the Communist party on the people and in consolidating his own hold on the party. Through him, the Communist party was to justify its use of such tactics as essential to eliminate all domestic opposition and to ward off any real or imagined threat to its rule from without the country.

Under Stalin, the Soviet Union was transformed into a world power. A nation that was predominantly agricultural at the time of the Bolshevik seizure of power emerged on the world scene as an industrial giant. Many people throughout the world see only this fact and accept it as evidence of the capability of the Communist system. They fail to look closely at the methods used by the system or to measure the cost in terms of human life and individual freedom by which the Soviet Union became a world power in a relatively short period of time. If they were to do so, they could well understand how Stalin's successor, Nikita S. Khrushchev, was able to document with specific and detailed examples his charges in 1956 that Stalin had been a murderer and a pathological liar who dealt in mass terror.

The question which naturally arises from Khrushchev's disclosures is: Why did Khrushchev, who rose to his own position of power under Stalin's tutelage and with his approval, wait until three years after Stalin's death to protest the inhumanities of which he was cognizant and in which he also was implicated? The question is largely answered by the fact that Khrushchev is as much a product of the system as Stalin was.

The Soviet Union's rapid emergence as a leading world power under communism was achieved by a ruthless dictator who used Marxism-Leninism as a theoretical justification for waging a campaign of terror marked by total disregard of traditional moral values and utter contempt for the cost in terms of human life and individual freedom.

Power Struggle

Even prior to Lenin's death in 1924, maneuvering had begun among the leading Bolsheviks for the position of supreme power in the Soviet Union. Lenin's health had begun to fail in 1921, and he had been forced to curtail his activities. A ruling triumvirate took over the reins of party leadership. It consisted of Joseph Stalin, who by 1922 had capped a long revolutionary career in support of Bolshevik efforts to seize power with his appointment to the position of general secretary of the party; Grigori Zinoviev, head of the Petrograd party organization and chief of the Third (Communist) International, commonly known as the Comintern; and Leo Kamenev, head of the Moscow soviet, or council. The three had joined forces against Lenin's heir apparent, Leon Trotsky.

Stalin's role as general secretary of the Communist Party of the Soviet Union placed him in a most advantageous position in the struggle for power that was to ensue. He already had begun to fill important party and government positions with his own men. Lenin originally had recommended that, after his death, party leadership be shared by Stalin and Trotsky. Before he died, Lenin recognized that, in aiding Stalin's rise in the party, he had helped create a potential tyrant. Lenin broke with Stalin in the early part of 1923, and, in what is usually referred to as his testament, warned that Stalin had gained enormous power. Lenin questioned Stalin's ability "to use that power with sufficient caution."

But Stalin had grown too powerful to be stopped by a dying Lenin. Despite Lenin's warning, the triumvirate continued to direct Soviet policies after his death, with Stalin later gaining the upper hand because of his party position. He skillfully used the power of that position to eliminate his rivals.

In using his party position and the party apparatus to eliminate his rivals, Stalin established a pattern for aspiring successors. The pyramid-type structure of the Communist party as designed by Lenin has a built-in system which can result only in an internal power struggle in which one man ultimately achieves the apex of dictatorial rule. The pattern set by Stalin in climbing to the top of that structure involved a variety of tactics. He argued against the theories of his rivals; he played one against the other; and he schemed to destroy them politically and, if necessary, physically.

"Left Opposition" Destroyed

Stalin's chief rival for power after the death of Lenin was Leon Trotsky. During the latter part of 1924, Stalin launched a campaign of vilification against Trotsky in which Kamenev and Zinoviev figured prominently. By 1925, Stalin had succeeded in removing Trotsky from his position as commissar of war.

Concurrently, another split was developing among party leaders over the party's policies toward the peasants. During this period, Stalin believed it expedient to tolerate the rising influence of the kulaks, the well-to-do farmers, to whom limited concessions had been granted under the New Economic Policy (NEP). Stalin was supported in his attitude toward the kulaks by Nikolal Bukharin, the party's leading theoretician; Alexei Rykov, who succeeded Lenin as premier of the Soviet Union; and Mikhail Tomsky, head of the Soviet trade unions.

On the other hand, Zinoviev expressed the view that the NEP had been merely a tactical maneuver adopted by Lenin as a temporary expedient. Zinoviev contended that any policy which increased the influence of the peasants also decreased the influence of the industrial workers and was, therefore, a deviation from Marxism. Because of the militant proposals made by Zinoviev and his supporters in connection with his contention, they came to be known as the "left opposition" in the party.

The Fourteenth Party Congress

The argument regarding the status of the kulaks contained the seeds which Stalin cultivated to destroy his rivals in the triumvirate. He used the Fourteenth Congress of the Communist Party of the Soviet Union, held in 1925, as the setting for their downfall.

In preparation for the Fourteenth Congress, the Leningrad organization had elected a delegation which solidly backed Zinoviev. The Moscow party organization, under Stalin's influence, condemned this move. The Leningrad group retaliated with an attack on the Moscow group. The stage was set for a clash at the congress, and Stalin was ready when it convened.

Kamenev charged at the congress that Stalin was attempting to usurp complete authority in the party. The charge led to demonstrations against Kamenev by the delegates. When Zinoviev spoke, his remarks were met with insults and jeers. Stalin made the countercharge that he was attempting to undermine the collective leadership of the party.

Those seeking to re-create the scene can find its counterpart in recent Soviet history. A similar charge was made in a more recent struggle for power inside the Soviet Union. In 1957 and 1958, Nitkita S. Khrushchev used the same argument to denounce Soviet party leaders Georgi Malenkov, Vyacheslav Molotov, Lazar Kaganovich, Dmitri Shepilov, and Nikolai Bulganin as an "anti-party group" in his further drive for power after exposing Stalin's past deeds and destroying his previous image.

At the Fourteenth Congress, Zinoviev and Kamenev suffered an ignominious defeat. Kamenev was removed from most of his positions immediately. Those that he did retain he lost shortly thereafter. Zinoviev remained a member of the Politburo, the leading policy-making body of the party, now known as the Presidium. However, Zinoviev's influence was reduced when Stalin enlarged the Politburo and packed it with men loyal to him. Following the congress, Zinoviev was also stripped of his organizational support when Stalin forced through a complete reorganization of the Leningrad party.

Trotsky's Exile

Trotsky had remained aloof from the controversy. During 1925, he devoted most of his activities to administrative matters. In September of that year, he even supported Stalin briefly by falsely denying the existence of Lenin's testament when Lenin's warning about Stalin received publicity. But by the spring of 1926 Trotsky had aligned himself with the forces of the "left opposition" in opposing Stalin's policies.

The opposition group continued its attacks on Stalin's policies for approximately a year and a half. At the same time, Stalin was consolidating his control of the party organization. Finally, he was ready to make his move. In July, 1926, he had Zinoviev removed from the Politburo. Zinoviev and Trotsky later organized a series of public demonstrations and demanded full party discussion of the issues involved.

Stalin moved swiftly against his rivals. In October, 1926, Zinoviev was removed as chairman of the Comintern, and Trotsky and Kamenev were removed from their positions on the Politburo. Nor did Stalin let up once his opponents were on the run. The following year, both Trotsky and Zinoviev were expelled from the Central Committee of the party on charges that they were holding secret meetings and operating a secret printing press. In November of that year, both were expelled from the party. A month later, Kamenev also was expelled.

Stalin ruthlessly pressed his attack against Trotsky. In 1929, Trotsky was ordered to leave the Soviet Union. He was granted political asylum in Turkey and lived there until 1933, when he moved to France. He left there in 1935 and found refuge in Norway. In 1937, as a result of protests by the Soviet government, he was forced to leave that country and was granted asylum by Mexico. He lived in Mexico City until August, 1940, when a man, allegedly a Stalinist agent, drove an axe into his skull and caused his death. In May, 1960, the assassin, who had spent the intervening years in a Mexican jail in payment for his crime, was released from prison. On release, he was met by two representatives of the Communist Czechoslovak diplomatic corps in Mexico City and, reportedly, was escorted to Prague by way of Havana.

In his "secret speech" attacking Stalin in 1956, Khrushchev did not condemn him for destruction of the "left opposition" group. In fact, he praised him for the "positive role" he had played in eliminating "the enemies of Leninism." It was an "ideological fight," he explained, through which "the party became strengthened and tempered." Khrushchev had to take such a position, because condemnation of Stalin on that point would have been tantamount to condemnation of the Communist system itself. Khrushchev had to make it appear that the mass terror to which the Russian people had been subjected under Stalin's rule was not the fault of the system but of the man—of the "cult of the personality." Therefore, he was able to find justification for Stalin's subsequent liquidation of rivals who comprised a "right opposition" group.

"Right Opposition" Destroyed

After defeating the "left opposition" forces, Stalin adopted the program they had advocated. Thus, he put into practice the very same ideas which he had used as the basis for charges that his rivals were guilty of ideological deviations. In May, 1928, he announced his proposal for the rapid development of heavy industry in the Soviet Union, which he planned to finance by the forcible collectivization of agriculture. In advocating this program, he turned against the party leaders who had supported him in the fight against the "left opposition." Most prominent in this category were men like Bukharin, Tomsky, and Rykov. They and their supporters were to become identified as the "right opposition" group.

The "ideological deviation" of the "right opposition" group was based on its proposals for a more moderate program of industrialization. They recommended that light industry as well as heavy industry be developed, and they opposed the forcible seizure of land from the farmers.

The speed with which Stalin was to dispose of his rivals on the "right" was an indication of his own growing power. Bukharin attempted to solicit the support of Kamenev and Zinoviev, who had been readmitted to the party in the Summer of 1928, after Stalin succeeded in reducing them to political ineffectiveness. Bukharin feared that Stalin's adoption of the original ideas of Kamenev and Zinoviev might lead him to form a new liaison with them, and Bukharin hoped to enlist their support first.

Bukharin's efforts backfired when the nature of his contacts with Kamenev was exposed. In February, 1929, Bukharin, Tomsky, and Rykov were all ordered to explain their contacts with Kamenev. They countered by criticizing Stalin for attempting to impose his rule. They urged an end to the organization of the collective farms and called for a slower pace in the industrialization program. But the Politburo condemned their views, their contacts with Kamenev, and their factionalism.

Those who comprised the "right opposition" were in a vulnerable position. They had approved several resolutions affirming the unity of the party's leadership. Since they had been staunch supporters of Stalin and of the need for party discipline in the attack on the "left opposition," they were not in a position to defend themselves when the same type of attack was made against them. Moreover, the forces of the "right" had overestimated their strength. Now that they were accused of provoking factionalism, their only alternative was to avoid expulsion from the party in the hope that eventually they might be able to influence party policy from within.

But Stalin was determined to eliminate them. In June, 1929, Tomsky was replaced as head of the trade union organization. The following month, Bukharin was removed from his position as chairman of the executive committee of the Comintern. He was also accused of an attempt to form a faction with the "left opposition." Stalin launched the now-familiar campaign of vilification against him in the Soviet press.

Stalin stalked his rivals on the "right" as relentlessly as he had pursued those on the "left." By November, 1929, Bukharin, Rykov, and Tomsky made public confessions of their "errors." But their confessions were not accepted. Shortly thereafter, they published a declaration again admitting their guilt and pledging their efforts to insure support for party policies which, by then of course, were Stalin's policies.

With the capitulation of the "right opposition," Stalin's aim to eliminate his main rivals for power was achieved. But Khrushchev was to describe Stalin's actions in a different way in 1956. He explained that "both the Trotskyites and the rightist opportunists were politically isolated" as a result of Stalin's "positive role" and therefore "the party was able to awaken and organize the working masses to apply the Leninist party line and to build socialism." Thus, all of Stalin's tactics of playing rivals against each other, of manipulating the party apparatus, and of intrigue and even murder were justified by Khrushchev. In the Communist system, the struggle for power is disguised as an ideological controversy.

It required a great deal of distorted reasoning by Khrushchev to justify Stalin's crimes, but it is easy to see why he tried to do so. Six months after Stalin died in 1953, Khrushchev assumed the all-important position of leadership of the Communist Party of the Soviet Union. Georgi Malenkov, meanwhile, had assumed Stalin's position as head of the Soviet government. The seeds of a new power struggle had been planted. By 1955, Malenkov was removed. A major factor in his removal was the stress which he had placed on the production of consumer goods. His successor, Bulganin, announced that priority would be given to the continued expansion of heavy industry. Yet, in February, 1957, Khrushchev, who was soon to replace Bulganin as head of the Soviet government, presented a revised economic plan which provided for greater emphasis on the production of consumer goods and a reduction of industrial expansion.

Collectivization of Agriculture

When Stalin's defeat of the "left" and the "right" was completed, his authority was unquestioned. He abandoned the New Economic Policy and ordered a still more rapid pace of industrialization. Since there was little likelihood of attracting foreign investment to pay for the machinery needed, Stalin's alternative was to step up agricultural production with the hope of using increased grain exports to finance the importation of machinery. This new program was to prove disastrous for the kulaks, who had experienced a degree of independence under the NEP and who strongly resisted the agricultural policies of the Communist party.

In 1929, Stalin ordered the liquidation of the kulaks as a class. The war against them became, in effect, a war against all peasants. Local soviets were authorized to confiscate privately owned farms, to incorporate them into collective farms, and to deport the kulaks themselves.

When the local soviets showed some reluctance in enforcing these harsh measures, the task was assigned to the secret police, and they accomplished their assignment with brutal efficiency. Their ruthless tactics resulted in the collectivization of more than one half of the peasants within a five-month period. The peasants resisted by slaughtering their cattle and horses by the tens of thousands.

The peasants' opposition resulted in the use of a different tactic by Stalin. In March, 1930, he relaxed the collectivization drive and, at the same time, placed the blame for its severity on lower party officials whom he charged with being guilty of using excessively brutal tactics. As a result, the percentage of collectivized farms in the Soviet Union dropped from more than 50 per cent to around 20 per cent.

But Stalin was following the Communist tactic of taking one step back to take two steps forward. The collectivization campaign was soon resumed and pressed even harder. By the end of 1932, approximately 60 per cent of the peasants had been collectivized. The Communist regime decreed the death penalty for the theft of grain. Peasants who left the collectives lost the right to any land, and the penalties for speculation in farm products were stiffened.

As a result of Stalin's determination to push ahead with the collectivization program over the great opposition of the peasants, the Soviet Union was gripped by famine during 1932 and 1933. Intent on industrialization, Stalin callously sacrificed the well-being of the rural population in order to provide food for the workers in the cities. The limited food supply of the peasants was seized and rationed among the workers. Millions died as a result of the man-made famine which the Soviet Union refused to admit even existed.

In 1956, Khrushchev was to brush aside the millions of deaths that resulted from the famine. "Let us consider for a moment what would have happened," he said, if "orientation toward 'cotton-dress industrialization,' or toward the kulak" had prevailed. "We would not now have a powerful heavy industry, we would not have the Kolkhozes [collective farms], we would find ourselves disarmed and weak in a capitalist encirclement." Through the "inexorable ideological fight" which Stalin had conducted against all those who opposed the steps by which such accomplishments were achieved, Khrushchev declared, Stalin had made it possible for the Communist party "to awaken and organize the working masses to apply the Leninist party line and to build socialism." In other words, under the Communist system, a tactical move is good, even if it involves the death of millions in a man-made famine, as long as it results in the strengthening of the Communist party so that it can build the country into an international power.

Soviet Labor Policy

The ruthless exploitation of the Soviet people can be seen in the labor policies and labor laws which Stalin used to achieve his objective. Stalin was willing to starve the peasants to provide the workers with food, because Soviet national power depended upon the productivity of the proletariat. At the same time, Soviet policy toward labor was far from benevolent. The brutal measures applied against the peasantry had their counterparts in measures used against the workers.

Until 1928, mass unemployment had prevailed in the Soviet

Union under the Communist regime. The first Five Year Plan to increase industrial capacity went into effect that year, and, by the following year, shortages began to appear in the labor market. The sudden change was not the result of Communist efficiency. The labor shortage was due, to some extent, to the vast industrial expansion outlined in the first Five Year Plan, but other factors also contributed.

The collectivization program caused many temporary urban workers to return to their farms in the hope of protecting their agricultural holdings. It also deterred many peasants whose farms had not yet been collectivized from going to the cities for temporary employment, because of the risk that their farms would be expropriated in their absence.

The labor shortage was further aggravated by an extraordinarily high rate of turnover in industrial employment. This problem was caused by a decline in real wages, by an acute housing shortage in the cities, by inequality in wages in different industries, and by labor piracy, sometimes on a mass scale, engaged in by factory managers seeking to fulfill the production quotas assigned them under the Five Year Plan.

The assigning of unrealistic production quotas is a technique still in use in Communist countries. To this day, Soviet factory managers have to resort to all sorts of subterfuges, including falsification of records, in order to meet their unrealistic quotas.

Repression of the Workers

It quickly became apparent to Stalin that the labor shortage, combined with the high rate of labor turnover, was making it impossible to achieve the goals he had set for industrial expansion. Obviously, the most effective way to cope with the situation would have been to raise wages and improve the living and working conditions of the labor force. But Stalin attempted to solve the problem of labor turnover by introducing a series of measures which ostensibly preserved freedom in the choice of employment but actually abolished the freedom of the Soviet worker to leave his job.

Party-controlled trade unions pressured the workers to pledge to remain in their jobs for the duration of the Five Year Plan. Trade unions in a Communist society serve as instruments of the Communist regime to spur production and to enforce labor discipline. By contrast, trade unions in a free society have the right to bargain collectively with management to determine wages and working conditions.

In a step-by-step procedure, decrees were issued to diminish the worker's freedom and to bring him under tighter control of the state. In September, 1930, a decree was issued which denied all claims to unemployment benefits to workers who had terminated their employment "arbitrarily." Later, a law was passed that barred for six months from any job in industry or transportation all employees who left their jobs without notice, who had left their job more than once within a year, or who had been discharged for unjustified absence. By the end of 1932, employers were required to discharge workers who had been absent from work without a valid reason for as little as one day. The workers so discharged were deprived of their ration cards and evicted from the living quarters provided by the industry.

The eviction action was made even more repressive in 1933 when the government ruled that offenders could be evicted not only from housing owned by the industry but also from housing cooperatives in which they had been allotted space under an agreement with their employer. Since, for all practical purposes, there was no other housing available, this regulation meant that a worker and his family could find themselves homeless for as little as one day's unjustified absence from work.

In December, 1932, everyone in the Soviet Union was ordered to carry an identity card issued by the police. Since the date that an individual's employment began had to be entered on the identity card, it became another effective means for the regime to use in controlling the movement of the worker and, indirectly, in keeping him on his job.

To spur production, harsh measures which forced competition between workers and set extreme production quotas were introduced. These measures, along with incentives for workers, were all designed to speed up production and were glorified by the Communist regime which, at the same time, hurled charges at capitalist countries accusing them of exploiting the workers.

By 1933, unions had lost the right to participate in negotiations to determine the wages of their members. By that time, Soviet slave-labor camps, in which millions lived and worked under barbarous conditions, had become another aspect of life under communism.

In 1956, when Khrushchev tried to place all the blame on Stalin and not on the system, he necessarily failed because the man and the system were as one. It was inevitable that the system should produce such a man as Stalin. Khrushchev said:

> Stalin acted not through persuasion, explanation, and patient cooperation with people, but by imposing his concepts and demanding absolute submission to his opinion. Whoever opposed this concept or tried to prove his viewpoint, and the correctness of his position—was doomed. . . .

Khrushchev cannot shift the responsibility for the millions of farmers, peasants, and workers who met their doom under Stalin's rule.

Mass Terror

> Stalin . . . began to use mass terror against the party cadres.
>
> > Nikita S. Khrushchev, 1956.

The organized terror of the dictatorship of the proletariat was to serve Stalin well in eliminating those he considered rivals for power. At the height of the industrialization drive on December 1, 1934, the head of the Leningrad party organization, Sergei M. Kirov, was assassinated under mysterious circumstances. The incident served as an excuse for Stalin to launch a new drive to eliminate his rivals. Stalin himself interrogated the assassin. He and 13 alleged accessories, all described as "Zinovievites," were executed in late December, 1934.

Kirov, who had been a member of the Politburo, was probably regarded by Stalin as a potential threat to his leadership. In 1932, a group opposed to Stalin's policies had secretly prepared a program setting forth their views. When Stalin learned of it, he had asked the members of the Politburo, including Kirov, to approve the death penalty for some of the members of the group. But the Politburo refused Stalin's demand, and the penalties inflicted were prison sentences or exile. Subsequent events revealed that Stalin had not forgotten this defeat in the Politburo.

Kirov had been a friend of Leon Trotsky. From exile, Trotsky charged that the secret police undoubtedly had known of the plot to kill Kirov and that Stalin had been made aware of it before the assassination took place. Significantly, at the Twentieth Congress in 1956, Khrushchev included in his "secret speech" the following comment on the Kirov case:

It must be asserted that to this day the circumstances surrounding Kirov's murder hide many things which are inexplicable and mysterious and demand a most careful examination. There are reasons for the suspicion that the killer of Kirov, Nikolayev, was assisted by someone from among the people whose duty it was to protect the person of Kirov. A month and a half before the killing, Nikolayev was arrested on the grounds of suspicious behavior, but he was released and not even searched. It is an unusually suspicious circumstance that, when the Chekist assigned to protect Kirov was being brought for an interrogation, on 2 December 1934, he was killed in a car 'accident' in which no other occupants of the car were harmed. After the murder of Kirov, top functionaries of the Leningrad NKVD (secret police) were given very light sentences, but in 1937 they were shot. We can assume that they were shot in order to cover the traces of the organizers of Kirov's killing.

The assassination of Kirov unleashed a reign of terror. Many who formerly opposed Stalin, but who had confessed their errors and had been readmitted to the party, were suddenly expelled, arrested, imprisoned, or deported.

Among the first against whom action was taken were Zinoviev and Kamenev. On January 16, 1935, it was announced that they and other former oppositionists would be tried for falsely claiming to have abandoned their views and for directing a secret opposition center against the regime, thus indirectly causing Kirov's assassination. After a secret trial in January, 1935, they both were sentenced to prison. For the rest of that year, the party conducted a purge campaign to screen out undesirable elements and "enemies of the party."

Communist Purges

The following year marked the beginning of the "show trials." In these trials, which have become a feature of Communist "justice," the guilt of the accused was predetermined, and the courtroom drama served only as a forum to convey a propaganda message.

On August 19, 1936, Zinoviev, Kamenev, and 14 other defendants were arraigned on charges of organizing a "terrorist centre" under the leadership of the exiled Trotsky. The group also was charged with plotting acts of terrorism against various Soviet leaders, as well as with the actual assassination of Kirov. The fact that Zinoviev and Kamenev had been convicted and imprisoned the year before on substantially the same charges did not preclude the holding of a new trial.

All except one of the accused publicly admitted guilt. In fact, their confessions were practically the only evidence introduced against them. All of the 16 defendants were sentenced to death and shot immediately.

A second "show trial" was held in January, 1937. There were 17 defendants in this trial. They were charged with plotting terroristic acts, collaborating with the defendants in the first trial, and espionage. All of them "confessed"; 13 were sentenced to death; and the others received prison terms.

Another purge was used to liquidate the "enemies of the state" in the Soviet Army, Navy, and Air Force. In June, 1937, the Soviet press announced that a group of high-ranking military officers had been arrested and would be tried secretly. The charges on which they were arrested were never disclosed. The Soviet press reported that they had engaged in espionage on behalf of Germany and Japan.

The military purge lasted until the following year. When it finally was over, the majority of the Soviet marshals, generals, and colonels, and approximately 30,000 officers of lower rank had been killed. Stalin, in his obsession for total power, had crippled Soviet military leadership just one year before the outbreak of World War II.

The third "show trial" was held in March, 1938. There were 21 defendants in that trial, including the "right oppositionists" Bukharin and Rykov; Tomsky had committed suicide in 1936. In addition, the third "show trial" featured as one of the defendants the head of the secret police, Genrikh Yagoda, who had served Stalin so well by producing the "confessions" that formed the basis for the first two trials. Again, the defendants were charged with the usual crimes, and Trotsky was pictured as the real head of the conspiracy. Of the 21 defendants, 18 were sentenced to death and the three remaining received prison sentences, largely on the basis of their own confessions.

The net result of the reign of terror, marked by the almost endless trials both public and secret, was incredible. Stalin had executed or imprisoned 11 of the "men of October" who had played prominent roles in the Bolshevik seizure of power in 1917. With the exception of Trotsky, who was in exile, Stalin had purged all of his former associates who, with him, had been members of Lenin's Politburo.

The list of the victims of the trials was impressive. It included a former premier, many vice-premiers, several ambassadors and two former heads of the Comintern. Victims among the military included the chief of the general staff, the political commissar of the army, and the commanders of most, if not all, of the important military districts. And, for each individual who confessed at a public trial, there were thousands more who were summarily executed or sentenced to concentration camps without any public hearing but merely on the basis of questioning by the secret police.

Ironically, as early as 1904, Trotsky had predicted the final outcome when he criticized Lenin's concept of a highly centralized Communist party. Trotsky had prophesied:

> The organization of the party takes the place of the party itself; the Central Committee takes the place of the organization; and finally the dictator takes the place of the Central Committee. . . .

Once the Communist party, itself a minority dictatorship, had taken control of the government, there was no problem in justifying its minority dictatorship over the state. And, as Trotsky had predicted, the dictator (Stalin) had assumed the power of the Central Committee. When Stalin ended the purges in the late 1930's, he had established absolute control of an organization which had absolute control of the Soviet Union. He had wiped out all opposition—both actual and potential—and had restaffed his organization with intimidated subordinates, including Nikita S. Khrushchev, who directed the purge in the Ukraine.

Stalin stood alone and unchallenged, holding untrammelled power. He had consolidated the dictatorship of the proletariat. He had also enlarged the industrial base which was to be the springboard for the Soviet Union's rise to prominence as a world power. However, he had accomplished this through the use of brutal methods which completely disregarded the inherent dignity and worth of the individual and at a cost in terms of human suffering that can never be measured. In the process, Stalin established a pattern for the internal power struggles that are inevitable under the Communist system, as well as a pattern for the total regimentation of Communist regimes.

Part Four

World Expansion

Chapter 8

Adjunct of Soviet Policy

It would be impossible to count the millions of people throughout the world who have been deceived and betrayed by the Communists. Many have been deceived by Communist propagandists who have portrayed the counterfeit revolution through which the Bolsheviks seized power as a "glorious" mass uprising of the Russian people.

According to Marxist-Leninist principles, the revolution was supposed to mark the beginning of the transformation of the world from a group of so-called bourgeois nation-states into a single proletarian world society devoid of nationalistic differences. In their efforts to achieve such a transformation, Communists have succeeded in turning millions of people throughout the world into traitors to their own countries. They have done it by creating a new type of loyalty—allegiance to the Soviet Union. It is a loyalty that demands devotion to the Soviet Union as the birthplace of the "glorious" revolution of 1917. It is a loyalty that transcends national interests and replaces them with an alleged international interest.

The Communist leaders of the Soviet Union have used this unique brand of international loyalty to further their own national interests. They have done so by establishing the idea in the minds of their followers throughout the world that whatever serves to advance the interest of the Soviet Union also serves to advance the interest of communism. The traitorous aspect of this idea is inherent in and flows from the Communist code of morality which dictates that anything—even treason against one's country—is justified if it advances the cause of communism.

The loyalty of Communists the world over to the Soviet Union has been a factor in the rapid ascendancy of the Soviet Union to a position of power in international affairs. Without such support, the Soviet Union would have required a much longer time to make the industrial, scientific, and technological advances that have brought it to a position where it rivals the United States in such fields. In the United States alone, for example, Communists through the years have used any and every means, including espionage, to ferret out this nation's secrets and to turn them over to the Soviets.

The irony in all this is that the betrayers have themselves been betrayed. For, while these traitors throughout the world have been sacrificing everything to contribute to Soviet interests in the belief that they were advancing the cause of the proletariat in their own and other countries, the Communist leaders of the Soviet Union have time and again deliberately betrayed the interest of the international Communist movement when it served their national interest to do so.

Stalin imposed his rule on the Russian people and used them with a cruel disregard of human values and life itself to build the Soviet state into a powerful force on the international scene. In this chapter, it will be shown how the Communist Party of the Soviet Union was equally ruthless in its use of other Communist parties throughout the world to support Soviet policies and further Soviet interests.

For years, as the leading nation in the international Communist movement, the Soviet Union has commanded the allegiance and active support of Communist parties throughout the world and has made the international Communist movement, in effect, an adjunct of Soviet policy.

International Revolutionary Aims

Immediately after they seized power in Russia in 1917, the Communists began active preparations for the international revolution that was supposed to result in the establishment of a single world society. The immediacy of their preparations is shown by the fact that as early as December, 1917, the Soviet government appropriated 2,000,000 rubles "for the needs of the revolutionary internationalist movement."

One of the first international revolutionary efforts of the Communists was directed at Germany. That country and Russia had established diplomatic relations after World War I, and the Soviets had a diplomatic mission in Germany. However, the mission was much more than a diplomatic agency. Through it, funds and revolutionary propaganda material were being funneled by the Soviets to German Communists. In January, 1919, they made a bid to seize power in that country. But the attempt failed and resulted in the execution of the leaders of the German Communist movement.

Soviet leaders soon expanded their activities to include the United States. In 1920, for example, a Soviet courier was arrested in Berlin, Germany, and was found to be carrying a message meant for Communists in the United States. The content of the message was most revealing. It stated in part:

> ... the time is ripe to form a Communist Party of America, officially affiliated with the Communist International. ...
> Upon the formation of the Communist party, measures should be taken to have a representative at Moscow.
> Workers' soviets should on no account be allowed to develop into bodies for philanthropic or educative ends. We fear that in America a danger of this kind exists. We therefore insist that the soviets shall be fighting organizations for seizing control of the state, for the overthrow of government, and the establishment of the workers' dictatorship. This is their sole task. The leading of strikes, of unemployment agitation, and of insurrection—such must be their activity. ...
> Propagate with all possible force the idea of the arming of the workers. Let not demobilized revolutionary soldiers give up their rifles. ...
> Act centrally. Do not fall asunder. Organize conspirative revolutionary headquarters.

These revolutionary aims and activities were the result of planning taking place among leaders of the organization referred to in the message itself—the Communist International, or Comintern, as it is usually known.

The Comintern

As conceived by Lenin, the Comintern was to be the means through which he could reach out and impose communism on the world. Plans for its formation began in January, 1919, when the Soviet government issued invitations to a conference to be held in Moscow in March of that year for the purpose of organizing the Comintern, or the Third International.

Two major reasons lay behind the organization of the Comintern. First, Lenin was convinced that the new Communist government of Russia would fall unless successful Communist revolutions could be instigated in other nations, particularly in Western Europe.

Second, Lenin believed that the instigation of revolutionary action throughout the world depended upon the guidance of members of an organization bound together with a revolutionary creed. Lenin scorned the views of the Socialist elements which had earlier abandoned Marx' revolutionary program in favor of a program to achieve socialism by working within the framework of the capitalist system. In addition, Lenin was determined to frustrate plans of European Socialists to consolidate the fragmented international Socialist movement. Since some Socialists had been attracted to the Bolshevik cause, Lenin feared the loss of their support if the consolidation efforts of the European Socialists were successful.

The founding meeting of the Comintern was a contrived affair. Only 35 delegates and 15 observers, all carefully selected by the Soviets, attended the meeting. Grigori Zinoviev was elected president of the Comintern at this meeting. But behind the facade of his leading role stood Lenin, who was the guiding spirit of the organization.

It is significant that those Socialists in Germany who were regarded by Lenin as the most important factor in the spread of communism in Europe opposed the formation of the Comintern. They believed that its formation was premature because of the weakness of the revolutionary movement in Western Europe. They also feared that the formation of an international Communist organization at that early date would result inevitably in its domination by the Soviet Communist party. Their fears were borne out. The Communist revolutions in Western Europe did not occur, and the Soviet Union dominated the Comintern from its inception.

The 21 Conditions

In 1920, Lenin saw to it that the Comintern had the power to enable the Soviet regime to demand the unquestioned allegiance of Communists everywhere. The Second World Congress of the Comintern was held in Moscow that year and is of special significance because it laid down the organizational structure of the world Communist movement by adopting 21 conditions as requisites for membership in the Comintern. Drawn up by Lenin, the 21 conditions were broad and demanding. They also were skillfully designed to serve his immediate aims.

Lenin desired to use every possible means to disrupt opposition to the Soviet regime by other countries. He struck at this point in the fourteenth condition for membership which read:

> Each party desirous of affiliating with the Communist International should be obliged to render every possible assistance to the Soviet Republics in their struggle against all counter-revolutionary forces. The Communist parties should carry on a precise and definite propaganda to induce the workers to refuse to transport any kind of military equipment intended for fighting against the Soviet Republics, and should also by legal or illegal means carry on a propaganda amongst the troops sent against the workers' republics, etc.

In the sixteenth and twenty-first conditions for membership, Lenin achieved a dual purpose. On the one hand, he provided the means by which the Comintern was to be fashioned in the image of his Communist party—as a highly centralized and strongly disciplined organization. On the other hand, he succeeded in establishing conditions that would have a divisive effect on the Socialist movement throughout the world by making it impossible for Socialist groups to join the Comintern without losing their independence.

The sixteenth condition for membership read:

> All the resolutions of the congresses of the Communist International, as well as the resolutions of the Executive Committee are binding for all parties joining the Communist International . . .

And the twenty-first condition read:

> Those members of the party who reject the conditions and

the theses of the Third International, are liable to be excluded from the party.

The remaining 18 conditions for admission included stipula-
tions that important Comintern documents had to be published
by the parties affiliated; that all affiliated parties had to establish
both a legal and an illegal (underground) apparatus; and that
they had to infiltrate the armed forces of the countries in which
they were organized. Additional measures were adopted at subsequent congresses of the Comintern, such as the regulations that
delegates to Comintern congresses had to come uninstructed and
that the congresses of member parties had to be held after Comintern congresses. All were designed to insure that control of the
Comintern remained in Soviet hands and that Communist parties
throughout the world were modelled after the Communist Party
of the Soviet Union.

The Comintern and Communism in America

The effectiveness of the Comintern in establishing Soviet control and direction of Communist movements in other countries
can be seen in the origin of the Communist movement in the
United States. The success of the Bolshevik revolution of 1917
had provided the basis for developing a movement with Soviet
orientation. The movement was organized in Chicago, Illinois,
in September, 1919, when two Communist parties were formed.
The Communist Labor party was organized largely by native-
born Americans who had unsuccessfully attempted to take
over the Socialist party from within. The Communist Party of
America was formed largely by foreign-born members who had
left the Socialist party with the protest that its policies were not
sufficiently revolutionary. Efforts to unite the two parties failed,
mostly because the foreign-language element—particularly the
Russians—feared the loss of their influence in a unified party and
refused to make any concessions to the Communist Labor party.

The existence of two competing groups in the United States
was totally unsatisfactory to Comintern leaders in the Soviet
Union. In January, 1920, Zinoviev, chairman of the Comintern,
sent an official communication to both parties, stressing that the
Comintern "categorically insists" that it is "absolutely necessary"
to form a single party. Largely as a result of the Comintern's demands, transmitted by several ultimatums and visits to the United

ORIGIN AND CONTINUITY OF THE COMMUNIST PARTY, USA

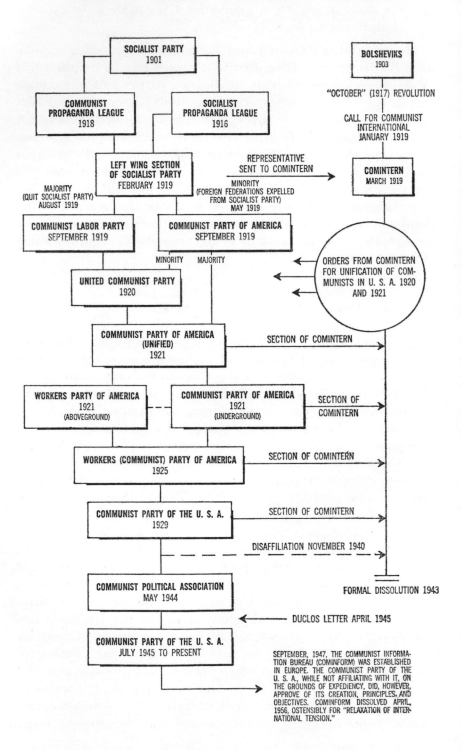

SEPTEMBER, 1947, THE COMMUNIST INFORMA-
TION BUREAU (COMINFORM) WAS ESTABLISHED
IN EUROPE. THE COMMUNIST PARTY OF THE
U. S. A., WHILE NOT AFFILIATING WITH IT, ON
THE GROUNDS OF EXPEDIENCY, DID, HOWEVER,
APPROVE OF ITS CREATION, PRINCIPLES, AND
OBJECTIVES. COMINFORM DISSOLVED APRIL,
1956, OSTENSIBLY FOR "RELAXATION OF INTER-
NATIONAL TENSION."

States by Comintern representatives, the two groups were finally merged in 1921.

Comintern Representatives

Comintern representatives, or "CI Reps" as they were familiarly known, had been used by the Soviets to direct Communist policies in this country as early as 1920. For years, the "CI Reps" were to play a dominant role in directing Communist activities here.

The power of the "CI Reps" in directing the affairs of the Communist Party, USA, was illustrated in the way in which they settled a leadership struggle within the party in 1929. Through the early period of the party's existence, a continuing struggle for power had taken place among the more prominent leaders of the Communist movement. By 1929, the leading contenders in the struggle were William Z. Foster and Jay Lovestone.

The leadership struggle was a major issue at the party's sixth convention, which was held in March, 1929. Lovestone seemed destined to be the winner in the struggle. He controlled an overwhelming majority of the delegates present.

The issue was decided, however, by the "CI Reps" who attended the convention. They had brought with them instructions from Moscow that Foster was to replace Lovestone as the general secretary of the party. Lovestone, they said, was to be assigned to work for the Comintern. The basic reason for Lovestone's ouster —his support of Bukharin's views—was frankly admitted by the "CI Reps." As mentioned previously, Stalin was at that time engaged in his ideological dispute with Bukharin and the other "right oppositionists."

American Exceptionalism

Another important reason for the Comintern's opposition to Lovestone was its condemnation of his theory of American exceptionalism. Lovestone had contended that there were unique characteristics in the political, social, and, particularly, the economic development of the United States. These characteristics, he had said, made the United States different from other capitalist nations. Therefore, he had concluded, Communist tactics which had been applicable to Western Europe would not necessarily be effective in the United States.

The Comintern's ouster of Lovestone from his leadership position is significant in two respects. First, it illustrates how Communist parties in other countries were prevented from following an independent course in their efforts to establish communism in their respective countries. They were forced to conform to the pattern established by the Soviets. Second, it shows how Communist parties in other countries were affected by the so-called ideological struggles of the Communist Party of the Soviet Union. As Stalin veered from position to position ideologically in his relentless purges of party rivals for power, leaders of Communist parties in other countries often found themselves purged if they did not veer ideologically with Stalin's sudden shifts.

Not to be overlooked in the importance of the role of "CI Reps" in this country is the clandestine nature of many of their activities. "CI Rep" J. Peters, for example, was acting head of the underground section of the Communist party in the United States in the early 1930's, when he personally took control of the espionage activities of Whittaker Chambers. Chambers later admitted that he had been a Communist agent. Peters had served briefly as a minor official in the Hungarian Communist regime of Bela Kun in 1919. Through Peters and other "CI Reps" whose activities had an important effect on the early history of the Communist Party, USA, the Communist movement in this country received the indelible mark of direct Soviet control maintained by the Comintern over all member parties.

Withdrawal from the Comintern

The Communist party in the United States joined the Comintern in 1921, accepting fully the 21 conditions for membership, which included unqualified allegiance to the Soviet Union. The party remained a member of the Comintern until 1940 when it withdrew for tactical reasons. In that year, the Voorhis Act was enacted by the United States Congress, and one of its provisions was that any organization in this country which was engaged in political activity and was subject to foreign control had to register with the Attorney General of the United States. To avoid the act's provisions, the Communists held an emergency convention at which they voted to disaffiliate from the Comintern. However, in announcing its disaffiliation, the party reaffirmed its adherence to the Comintern's principles and programs and made it explicitly clear that it was withdrawing only because of the Voorhis Act.

Promoting International Revolution

When Lenin agreed to the terms of the treaty of Brest-Litovsk in 1918, he justified its acceptance by the argument that all problems involving Soviet foreign relations had to be resolved in terms of the exclusive objective of preserving and strengthening the Communist regime in the Soviet Union. This did not mean that Lenin had abandoned the goal of world revolution. He was prepared to establish diplomatic and trade relations with non-Communist governments where he believed it would be advantageous to the Soviet government to do so. But he was also prepared to support revolutionary activities in other countries. Lenin's tactics resulted in a two-pronged Soviet approach to relations with the non-Communist world. While the Soviet government was attempting to exploit any opportunity to divide the non-Communist nations through diplomatic maneuvering, it was, at the same time, promoting world revolution through the Comintern.

The Comintern quickly gained control over the Communist parties throughout the world, and it was not long before the international Communist movement was transformed into an adjunct of Soviet policy. There was, on occasion, an identity of interests between the Communist Party of the Soviet Union and Communist parties in other countries. But whenever there was a conflict between them, Soviet interests prevailed.

In 1921, for example, the Soviet Union signed a Treaty of Friendship with Turkey, despite the fact that the Turkish government was embarked on a program designed to repress all Communist activities in that nation. In April, 1922, the Soviet Union and Germany signed a political and commercial alliance designed to strengthen both nations against the victorious allied powers of World War I. While Germany was anti-British and anti-French, the Comintern instructed German Communists to promote German nationalism, which had been inflamed by the French occupation of the Ruhr in January, 1923. However, in August, 1923, when the German government was replaced by one which sought greater cooperation with the West, Soviet leaders became convinced that this would lead to a shift in German foreign policy detrimental to Soviet interests. Accordingly, Comintern strategy changed, and German Communists were instructed to prepare for a revolutionary seizure of power. When the signal for the uprising was finally received from Moscow in October, 1923, the German Communists began an ill-timed revolt which was quickly suppressed.

Socialism in One Country

The policy of placing Soviet state interests above all others was to be greatly intensified by Stalin after Lenin's death. The struggle Stalin had won over Trotsky and others whom he considered rivals for power had taken the form of an ideological dispute. Of major importance was the difference in Trotsky's theory of "permanent revolution" and Stalin's theory of "socialism in one country."

Trotsky's theory called for immediate revolutions in other countries. Without widespread revolution, Trotsky maintained, the Soviet Union could not achieve communism, because of its lack of industrial development. He advocated using the Bolshevik revolution of 1917 as the spark with which to kindle proletarian revolutions in other nations, particularly in Western Europe, in an attempt to establish communism immediately on an international scale.

Stalin insisted that communism must first be made secure in the Soviet Union. He argued that it could be achieved through the development of the country's natural assets, and that, once achieved, the Soviet Union would then stand as the firm base from which revolutionary efforts could be directed and supported to establish world-wide communism.

Obviously, the goal of both theories was the same—the establishment of a world Communist society. They differed only in the method through which it was to be achieved. Stalin's view was more in keeping with a developing spirit of Soviet nationalism.

Stalin's victory over his rivals for power established his theory of "socialism in one country" as the cornerstone of future Soviet strategy. It served as the justification of demands that all other

Communist parties consider the defense of the Soviet Union as their paramount task. In 1927, for example, Stalin proclaimed:

> A revolutionary is he who without arguments, unconditionally, openly and honestly. . . . is ready to defend and strengthen the USSR, since the USSR is the first proletarian, revolutionary state in the world. . . . An internationalist is he who unreservedly, without hesitation, without conditions, is ready to defend the USSR because the USSR is the base of the world revolutionary movement, and to defend, to advance this revolutionary movement is impossible without defending the USSR.

At the same time, Soviet propagandists worked to convince Communists in other countries that Soviet policies were not based on national interests. Typical was the claim of the Comintern in 1927 that "nothing is Russian in the Soviet Union in the 'national' meaning of the word, everything is proletarian, that means: international."

The truth is so far from the claim that it borders on the ridiculous. The truth is that the international Communist movement was quickly transformed into an adjunct of Soviet policy.

This truth is best illustrated by the drive launched in 1928 by the international Communist movement against what it called "social fascism." This offensive, actually an outgrowth of Stalin's struggle to eliminate his "right-wing" rivals in the Soviet Union, was an attempt to identify the aims of the Socialists with fascism. In response to instructions from the Comintern, Communist parties throughout the world began a concerted attack against Socialist parties. The economic crises threatening many countries at that time had led Stalin to predict that the downfall of capitalism was imminent, and this world-wide Communist revolutionary offensive was launched in support of his prediction.

While ostensibly directed at furthering the interests of international communism, Stalin's grand strategy was nothing more than a cover for his personal interests. It will be recalled that, after he had eliminated his opposition on the "left," he had turned his attention to eliminating the opposition on the "right." To provide himself with ideological justification for veering off in an opposite direction, as well as for the extreme measures he was to resort to in building "socialism in one country," Stalin gave the signal that started the world Communist movement on an attack against "social fascism."

Communism and the Nazis

Communists in other countries blindly followed Stalin's directions. Their unquestioning obedience to Moscow was to have tragic consequences not only for many of the Communist parties but also for the world. In Germany, for example, the Nazis, under the leadership of Adolf Hitler, were gradually gaining strength. Although the combined strength of the German Communists and Socialists was almost double that of the Nazis at the time, the German Communists, in line with the Comintern's directions, refused appeals by the Socialists to form a united front against the Nazis. Instead, the German Communists began attacking the German Socialists.

Even when Hitler seized power in 1933 and began to suppress opposition groups, the German Communists continued their divisive attacks on the Socialists. Convinced that Hitler's regime was doomed to failure and was merely a prelude to their own seizure of power, German Communists saw Hitler as a weapon through which they could destroy the Socialists.

Hitler not only destroyed the Socialists, he also destroyed the German Communist party. In blindly following the Comintern's policies, the German Communists had contributed to their own destruction. In addition, by fostering such a situation in support of his own drive for power in the Soviet Union, Stalin contributed not only to the growth of a Nazi force that was to create havoc throughout the world but also to the growth of a tyrant as treacherous as himself—a tyrant who later was to threaten the very existence of the Soviet Union.

By 1934, the Nazi threat to the Soviet Union was all too apparent to Stalin and dictated a new course of foreign policy. The Soviet Union joined the League of Nations in September, 1934, and began efforts to improve Soviet relations with the West. This resulted in the signing of treaties with France and Czechoslovakia by May, 1935.

United Front Against Fascism

The change in Soviet foreign policy again dictated a change in the tactics of world communism. In 1935, the Seventh World Congress of the Comintern decreed that all Communist parties should adopt a united front against fascism. The Soviet appeal for unity against fascism was aimed at all segments of society which the Communists felt would be opposed to fascism. Moreover, it was an appeal that could be focused on any issue—economic, social, political, or cultural—just as long as it coincided with the national interest of Soviet policies in opposing fascism.

Under this application of the united-front tactic (also described as the popular or people's front), almost every existing organization of any type immediately became a target for Communist infiltration. For the first time, for instance, the Communists in the United States were able to join forces with such diverse groups as charitable and relief agencies, veterans' organizations, scientific societies, fraternal and civic groups, women's leagues, and consumer cooperatives. Special efforts were made to apply united-front tactics to racial, religious, and nationality groups.

In fields where no group existed which was susceptible to infiltration, the Communist Party, USA, quickly moved to organize one. Here, one of the prime targets of the new united-front tactic was the "intellectuals." The term "intellectuals" was used by the Communists to mean teachers, writers, artists, scientists, and entertainers.

Through the united-front tactic, the Communists were able to gain the cooperation of thousands of people throughout the world in support of the fight against fascism. Communist propagandists have since played up the "heroic struggle" of the world Communist movement in its fight against Hitler. But they gloss over the major contribution made by Stalin toward the development of fascism in the world. Most of all, they cover up the fact that the efforts of Communist parties throughout the world were dictated solely by their pledge of allegiance to Moscow and by their determination to protect the Soviet Union. Finally, they do their utmost to conceal how effectively all the Communist parties of the world had been manipulated by both Lenin and Stalin to transform Communist parties into nothing less than self-sacrificing adjuncts of Soviet policy.

Chapter 9

Communist Imperialism

In studying communism, it is essential to recognize that the world-wide Communist movement now constitutes the greatest imperialistic force of all time.

Communist imperialism is inherently insatiable. Acceptance of the Marxist principle that communism must be established on a world-wide scale binds Communists to a course of action which demands that they constantly exert pressure on non-Communist nations in order to prepare the way for communism's so-called inevitable triumph. Communists employ methods and practices which touch on every aspect of man's existence. The pressures they apply vary in type and intensity, but combine to represent a form of total imperialism which is new and unique in the nature of its challenge to the rest of the world.

Communists have committed themselves to a revolutionary doctrine which demands that they pursue a fixed goal through flexible methods. They are committed to relentless attacks on non-Communist nations, seeking continually to create disorder, confusion, and chaos. Through such tactics, Communists have created an empire—an empire built on human misery and suffering.

In November, 1917, the Bolsheviks took advantage of the chaos resulting from Russia's involvement in World War I, the weakness of the Provisional Government, and their own superior organization and discipline to impose a counterfeit revolution on the Russian people. Social and political upheaval, weakness of anti-Communist forces, and superior organization and discipline have been the ingredients of subsequent Communist successes which have led to Communist domination of one-third of the world's population.

Of all the nations now under Communist control, only Czechoslovakia enjoyed for any extensive period a democratic form of government before Communists seized power. In every other instance, communism has gained power in nations characterized by either a low level of economic and social development or a lack of political freedom, or both. Communism has had little success in those nations in which political democracy, economic progress, and social justice prevail.

Communism, an inherently imperialistic force, pursues a fixed goal through flexible methods and feeds on political, social, and economic upheaval to create and take advantage of chaos.

It has been shown how the Soviet Union became the acknowledged leader of the world Communist movement. Having established an international apparatus under the Comintern and having achieved an industrial base under Stalin, the Soviet Union was in a position to instigate or exploit situations of political, social, and economic upheaval outside its borders, and to assist Communist parties in other countries to achieve power.

"Capitalist Encirclement"

During the first years of Communist rule in Russia, the positive direction and control of the international Communist movement which Soviet leaders achieved through the Comintern contrasted sharply with the relatively defensive posture which the new Soviet state was forced to adopt in its foreign policy.

Stalin explained the defensive policies of the Soviet Union prior to World War II in terms of the theory of "capitalist encirclement." This theory held that the Soviet Union, as the only Socialist country, existed as an island surrounded and threatened by hostile capitalist nations intent on its destruction. Thus, said Stalin, a defensive posture was necessary until the Communists had consolidated their power and had transformed the Soviet Union into an industrial nation. However, once Stalin's unquestioned rule had been established and the Soviet Union had been launched on the path toward industrial development, Stalin took the offensive in exploiting situations favorable to the extension of communism beyond the boundaries of the Soviet Union.

Spanish Civil War

One of the first opportunities to exploit political and social upheaval abroad arose in Spain. When a civil war broke out in that country in 1936, the Communists acted in line with the theory that the Soviet Union should be used as the base for the extension of Communist control over other countries.

Soviet intervention in the Spanish civil war was twofold in nature. First, in response to directions from the Comintern, the international Communist movement organized International Brigades to fight in Spain. Typical was the Abraham Lincoln Brigade, organized in the United States. It succeeded in recruiting about 3,000 men. In all, the Communist parties of 53 countries were represented in the International Brigades with a total fighting strength of approximately 18,000, the first of whom arrived in Spain during the latter part of 1936. Second, the Soviet Union furnished direct military assistance in the form of tanks, artillery, and aircraft flown by Soviet pilots.

For two years, Moscow pursued its objectives in the Spanish struggle. However, Soviet intervention ended in the fall of 1938, when the national interests of the Soviet Union forced it to turn its attention elsewhere. In Europe, Hitler's strength was steadily increasing. In addition, Japan's armed invasion of Manchuria posed a direct threat to Soviet territory in the Far East. At the end of 1938, the International Brigades withdrew from Spain. Many Communists throughout the world who answered the Comintern's call to fight in Spain were repaid subsequently by Soviet assistance in their attempts to seize power in their respective countries. Among those identified with Communist efforts in connection with the Spanish civil war who subsequently gained prominence in the Communist movement were Tito (Yugoslavia), Palmiro Togliatti (Italy), Jacques Duclos (France), Klement Gottwald (Czechoslovakia), Erno Gero and Laszlo Rajk (Hungary), and Walter Ulbricht (East Germany).

Nazi-Soviet Pact

While communism and fascism had been on opposite sides during the Spanish civil war, this did not deter the Soviet Union from signing a nonaggression pact with Nazi Germany in August, 1939. The Soviet Union was interested, of course, in preventing a possible attack by Germany. But the pact was far more than a defensive measure. It was also a "treaty of aggression" for the Soviet Union and Nazi Germany.

For Hitler, it meant that he could attack Poland with the assurance that, if England and France came to her defense, he could wage war in Western Europe without fear of an attack from the east by the Soviet Union. For Stalin, it meant a free hand to exploit conditions in eastern Poland and in the Baltic nations. After Germany invaded Poland from the west on September 1, 1939, the Soviet Union, under cover of the nonaggression pact, invaded from the east on September 17, 1939, and annexed the eastern half of Poland.

The Baltic Area

The Soviet Union invaded Finland on November 30, 1939. A pretext for this move had been engineered by the Soviets when they set up in a Soviet border town a puppet "revolutionary Finnish government" headed by the Finnish Communist Otto Kuusinen. Significantly, Kuusinen was later to become a member of the Presidium of the Communist Party of the Soviet Union. Although the Finns resisted heroically, they were finally forced to cede some border territory to the Soviet Union by a peace treaty signed on March 12, 1940.

During the months of September and October, 1939, Latvia, Lithuania, and Estonia had been pressured into signing mutual assistance treaties with the Soviet Union. These treaties opened the door for Communist infiltration of the governments and armed forces of these Baltic countries. Finally, in June, 1940, after France had fallen to the Nazis, the Soviet Union served ultimatums on Latvia, Lithuania, and Estonia that governments friendly to the Soviet Union be established and that Soviet troops occupy these nations. Even before the Baltic nations capitulated to these ultimatums, the Soviet Army had invaded them and set up puppet governments.

"Elections" were held in these Baltic nations in July, 1940, after all non-Communist candidates were forced to withdraw or were ruled ineligible. In each of these Baltic countries, the Communist-front political parties were "elected." On July 21, 1940, the government of each country voted in favor of incorporating itself in the Soviet Union. This pattern of ruthless Communist imperialistic expansion through the use of various methods to supplant existing political regimes was to be used again, but in a more sophisticated manner, in Eastern Europe following World War II.

The Great "Patriotic" War

The Nazi-Soviet alliance was shattered on June 22, 1941, when German armed forces attacked the Soviet Union. The invasion brought the imperialistic ventures of the Soviet Union to a sudden, but temporary, halt.

The initial success of the smashing German attack placed the future of the motherland of the international Communist movement in grave jeopardy. Communist parties everywhere, which until then had been supporting the Nazis and disrupting the defense efforts of the Allies, rallied to the defense of the Soviet Union by switching tactics overnight.

For the first year and a half, the war went badly for the Soviet Union. Ironically, Communist leaders had to appeal to an instinct they allegedly scorned—the nationalism of the people. Responding to patriotic appeals to defend their country—not communism—the Soviet people endured incredible hardships in an effort to slow the advance of the German juggernaut.

Bolstered by huge quantities of war equipment and material provided by the United States through lend-lease, the Soviet people slowly turned the tide. In dire need of such assistance, Communist leaders of the Soviet Union even went so far as to dissolve the Comintern in 1943 to promote wartime unity. The Comintern, the tangible organizational structure of the international Communist movement, had long been an irritant to all non-Communist nations. However, its dissolution was merely a tactical gesture.

The turning point of the war in the Soviet Union occurred in January, 1943. The Soviet Army surrounded Stalingrad (now known as Volgograd) and the German forces there surrendered. Slowly, the Nazi forces were driven westward. At the same time,

UNITED STATES PROVIDED SOVIET UNION WITH HUGE QUANTITIES OF WAR EQUIPMENT AND MATERIALS VIA LEND-LEASE DURING WORLD WAR II.

$11,141,470,000 TOTAL VALUE

TANKS	AIRPLANES	TRACTORS
7,000	14,000	8,000
MACHINE GUNS	**MACHINERY**	**MERCHANT SHIPS**
135,000	$1,000,000,000	100
ANTIAIRCRAFT GUNS	**LOCOMOTIVES**	**TORPEDO BOATS**
8,000	2,000	200
EXPLOSIVES	**FREIGHT CARS**	**SUBMARINE CHASERS**
300,000 TONS	10,000	100
TRUCKS	**RAILROAD WHEELS AND AXLES**	**MARINE DIESEL ENGINES**
400,000	100,000 TONS	8,000
JEEPS	**RAILS**	**CHEMICAL PRODUCTS**
50,000	500,000 TONS	600,000 TONS
MOTORCYCLES	**FIELD TELEPHONES**	**COTTON AND WOOLEN CLOTH**
35,000	400,000	150,000,000 YDS.
TIRES	**TELEPHONE WIRE**	**ARMY BOOTS**
17,000,000	1,250,000 MILES	15,000,000 PRS.

Stalin instituted a program of severe reprisals against national minority groups living in the areas retaken. In 1944, entire national minority groups were uprooted and deported to Siberia. A new wave of Communist tyranny and terror was in the offing.

The European Satellites

Stalingrad not only marked the turning point in Soviet fortunes in World War II, it also marked the beginning of the Communist offensive in which seven European nations lost their freedom and were eventually transformed into "people's democracies." This was accomplished against the will of the people in each country and despite pious protestations by the Soviets that they were interested only in liberating these nations from Nazi domination.

In all these nations, with the exceptions of Yugoslavia and Albania, both of whom owed little to the Red Army in the establishment of their Communist regimes, the pattern of Communist expansion was similar. Two factors were common to the Communist seizures of power in Poland, Bulgaria, Rumania, Hungary, and Czechoslovakia. The first—and the most important—was the presence within these nations, in overwhelming strength, of the Red Army, which backed terroristic and subversive activities carried out by local Communists. The second was the presence of well-organized Communist groups under the leadership of native Communists who had spent considerable time between World War I and World War II in the Soviet Union, working closely with and under the direction of the Kremlin. During 1944 and 1945, these expatriate Communists—Georgi Dimitrov of Bulgaria, Matyas Rakosi of Hungary, Boleslaw Bierut of Poland, Klement Gottwald of Czechoslovakia, and Ana Pauker of Rumania—became leading figures in the provisional governments established in their war-ravaged nations in those chaotic years.

The tactics used by the Communists to seize control were aptly described by the Hungarian Communist leader Matyas Rakosi, who referred to them as "salami tactics." By this he meant that the Communists gradually sliced away at other political groups until, finally, all opposition was eliminated.

In this process, non-Communist political parties were forcibly incorporated in coalitions dominated by Communists; non-Communist leaders were arrested, imprisoned, refused permission to return from abroad, or deported; the non-Communist press was censored; non-Communist parties were infiltrated and disrupted from within; Communists gained control of key ministries (usually the ministries of Interior, Justice, and Communications) which gave them authority over the police and the media of communications; elections were rigged; and riots, strikes, and other demonstrations were organized to promote further unrest. In all these activities, local Communists were supported by the Red Army.

Communist territorial expansion following World War II extended as far west as Germany. Initially, Soviet personnel occupied the eastern portion of Germany while the United States, Great Britain and, somewhat later, France occupied western Germany under the terms of an agreement worked out by the nations which had defeated Germany. The agreement provided that all of Germany would remain a political and economic entity during the period of occupation which was to last until the signing of a peace treaty. But once the Soviet forces had taken up occupation of the eastern sector of Germany, Communist imperialism followed its now-familiar pattern. The agreement that Germany was to be dealt with as an entity was broken; factories were dismantled and transported to the Soviet Union; all non-Communist opposition was effectively suppressed; German Communists were installed in a puppet regime; and the East German Democratic Republic was established as another satellite.

The agreement for the occupation of Germany had also provided that the Soviet Union, Great Britain, and the United States would occupy separate sectors of the capital city of Berlin located in eastern Germany. (Later, Great Britain and the United States divided their sectors with France.) The Soviets made their sector the capital of the East German Democratic Republic. Then, in 1948, the Soviets attempted to extend their control over the entire city of Berlin by cutting off access rights of the Western occupying powers. This attempt was thwarted by a spectacular American and British airlift which lasted almost a year and provided the inhabitants of West Berlin with over a million and a half tons of supplies.

In the period immediately following World War II, Communist imperialism had seized control of seven nations in Europe. As these so-called "people's democracies" developed, they imitated the political, economic, and social life of the Soviet Union. They subordinated their national interests to the needs and interests of the "socialist camp" as dictated by the Soviet Union and, in 1955, united militarily with the Soviet Union in the Warsaw Pact. Communist imperialistic expansion in Europe had taken place despite Stalin's wartime pledge to "Liberate the peoples of Europe from the fascist invaders . . ." and grant them "the full right and freedom to decide for themselves the question of their form of government. . . ."

The Mediterranean Area

As World War II drew to a close, the Soviet Union made a determined effort to gain a political and economic foothold in North Africa and the Middle East. Soviet demands for trusteeships over Libya or the region of Tripolitania were rejected by the Allies when Soviet aggression in Europe clearly revealed Communist expansionist intentions.

Turkey, supported by extensive United States military aid, rejected Soviet demands for military bases in the strategic Dardanelles and for the annexation of territory in northeastern Turkey. Only after strong Western political pressure did the Soviet Union withdraw her troops from Iran in 1946. Iran was then able to eliminate the Communist-dominated, pro-Soviet regimes which had earlier been established in two northern regions of that country.

Greek Communists instigated three armed revolts during the period from 1943 to 1949 in an effort to gain power. In their final attempt, which began in 1946, the Communist rebels executed over 3,500 noncombatants, destroyed more than 11,000 homes, and looted nearly 7,000 villages. Their terrorist tactics forced some 700,000 persons to abandon their homes and seek refuge in safe areas. Finally, the Communist rebels abducted over 28,000 children (five to eight years of age) and forcibly removed them from Greece to various Communist nations. During this rebellion, the Communist governments in Albania, Yugoslavia, and Bulgaria furnished the Greek Communists war material; allowed them to use their territories for refuge; aided them in guerrilla recruitment; supported their rebellion over state-controlled radios; and facilitated their return to Greece after rest and medical treatment. Extensive American military and economic aid contributed materially to the ultimate defeat of the Communist rebels.

China

While the imperialist expansion of communism was taking place in Europe during and after World War II, additions to the Communist empire resulted from conquest in Asia. In China, communism dates back to July, 1921, when a small group, including Mao Tse-tung, met in Shanghai at a special founding conference. The following year, the Chinese Communist party joined the Comintern. In 1923, the Comintern instructed the Chinese Communist party to join in a coalition with the Kuomintang, and in January, 1924, Mao Tse-tung represented the Communist party at the First National Congress of the Kuomintang, held in Canton. The Kuomintang was the nationalist party in the Chinese Republic, organized in 1912. It had gained control of most of China by the late 1920's.

In 1927, the Communists revolted against the Kuomintang government. This revolt lasted uninterruptedly for 10 years, until the Japanese invasion from Manchuria brought about a temporary truce in 1937. One of the outstanding events of this 10-year period was the "long march" by the Communists. Following a series of "annihilation campaigns," which lasted from December, 1930, to October, 1934, and resulted in a crushing defeat for the Communist armies, Mao and approximately 100,000 of his followers started a 6,000-mile retreat to northwestern China. There was bitter fighting along the way, and fewer than 35,000 arrived at the final destination in Shensi Province.

The temporary truce between Mao and Chiang Kai-shek, leader of the Kuomintang, was ended by 1940, and there were occasional armed clashes between the two forces.

The Japanese surrender in 1945 found the Kuomintang (or Nationalist) troops located in the southern part of China. Communist troops were in the northern part, where they were being supplied with captured Japanese equipment by Russian occupation troops in Manchuria. A dispute developed between Mao Tse-tung and Chiang Kai-shek as to the composition of the postwar government and, when the Soviet Union withdrew from Manchuria in early 1946, there was a resumption of full-scale civil war.

The Nationalist forces were largely victorious during the remainder of 1946 and through 1947, but 1948 brought a reversal of fortunes. The Communists swept south, and the Nationalist government was forced to withdraw to the offshore island of

Formosa on December 8, 1949. In the meantime, on October 1, 1949, Mao Tse-tung had proclaimed the establishment of the People's Republic of China.

Korea

The Soviet Union declared war on Japan on August 8, 1945, or just before the end of World War II. Both American and Soviet troops participated in the surrender of the Japanese troops in Korea. The United States accepted the surrender south of the 38th parallel, which had been selected as an arbitrary dividing line. There was a clear-cut agreement that the Soviets would withdraw from Korea as soon as a national government was established. It was soon apparent that in Korea, as in Germany, the Soviet Union had no intention of permitting unification. On May 10, 1948, an election, limited to South Korea, was held because the Soviet Union refused to allow the United Nations Temporary Commission in Korea to enter North Korea.

A People's Democratic Republic of Korea was formed in North Korea in 1948. The Soviet Union reported that it had withdrawn its occupation forces by the end of 1948, but the United Nations commission was not permitted to verify this claim. On June 25, 1950, without any warning, North Korean armed forces invaded South Korea. Led by Soviet-made tanks, the North Korean infantry achieved complete tactical surprise.

On the same day, the United Nations Security Council adopted a resolution which called for immediate cessation of hostilities and withdrawal of North Korean forces. It requested all member nations to render assistance in the execution of this resolution. The United States began to furnish military assistance on June 27, 1950. By the end of October, United Nations forces had advanced to the Manchurian border. On November 4, 1950, General Douglas MacArthur, commander of the United Nations forces, reported that Chinese Communist forces had intervened in Korea. The Chinese Communists contended that these forces were "volunteers." This bitter military conflict lasted until the signing of a truce on July 27, 1953.

It is estimated that the Korean War brought death to over a million Koreans, 54,000 Americans, and thousands of soldiers from other United Nations countries which participated. Material destruction was estimated to be more than $5,000,000,000.

French Indochina

Communist activities in Indochina were led by Nguyen Tat Thanh, better known as Ho Chi Minh. Taking advantage of the unsettled conditions during World War II, this Moscow-trained Communist organized a guerrilla force to fight the Japanese. With the support of more than 10,000 guerrilla fighters, who were known as the Vietminh, a so-called Democratic Republic of Vietnam in Northern Indochina was established in September, 1945, with Ho Chi Minh as president.

Previously, Indochina had consisted of four French protectorates and the colony of Cochin China. The French agreed with the demands of Ho Chi Minh that Laos and Cambodia each be granted individual status but refused to merge the territories of Tonkin, Annam, and Cochin China into a single area to be known as Vietnam. When negotiations collapsed in the latter part of 1946, war broke out between the French and the Communist Vietminh.

During this war, France granted independence to Cambodia and Laos. At the end of the war in 1954, the 17th parallel was established as the border between Communist North Vietnam and South Vietnam. North Vietnam has since served as a base for guerrilla warfare against the governments of Laos and South Vietnam.

Communist Defeats in Southeast Asia

Elsewhere in Asia, similar Communist attempts to gain power by armed warfare were defeated. In the Philippine Islands, Communists who had been active in the resistance against the Japanese held out in the mountains following World War II. For approximately six years after the war, the "Huks," as they were known, looted and terrorized large areas of the country. In 1951, however, the Philippine government began a vigorous military campaign against these Communist insurgents. Within a year, this military action, combined with a program of agrarian reform, had reduced the Communist rebels to small, isolated, ineffective groups.

Beginning in 1948, Communists, operating from the jungles of Malaya, raided mines, villages, and plantations and terrorized large portions of the country. British and other Commonwealth troops launched a military campaign against them. By the end of 1959, after more than 10 years of jungle warfare, the Communist rebels had been reduced to a handful confined to the border between Thailand and Malaya.

Communists also began a revolt in Burma in 1948. Again, it was a revolt characterized by wanton acts of violence against the civilian population. Although military action by the Burmese government exerted strong pressure on the rebel forces, sporadic guerrilla warfare continued between the Communists and the Burmese armed forces until the latter part of 1958. By then, arrests and surrenders had reduced the insurgents to a few small, impotent groups hiding in the countryside.

Cuba

Events in Cuba clearly illustrate that Communist imperialism has not overlooked the Western Hemisphere. The agent of Communist imperialism in Cuba, the Cuban Communist party, was formally established in 1925 and has been known as the Popular Socialist party since 1944. Under Juan Marinello, president, and Blas Roca, secretary general, the party weathered the many changes in Soviet policy and in the Cuban government's attitude toward it.

After the overthrow of the Batista government by Fidel Castro's forces in January, 1959, Communists were appointed to key posts in the new regime. During the first three months of the Castro regime, Communist party membership in Cuba increased rapidly. Since mid-1960, there has been a rapid build-up of Communist-bloc arms in Cuba, and Cuba has entered into a series of far-reaching trade, technical, and cultural agreements with Communist nations. However, Castro waited until December, 1961, to announce that he was a Marxist-Leninist and would remain one "until the last day of my life."

Lenin's Theory of Imperialism

The record of international communism outlined above illustrates that it has been able to advance its imperialistic designs by exploiting conditions in areas of the world characterized by a low level of economic and social development or by a lack of political freedom, or both. Ironically, international communism promises to liberate people in such areas from what it describes as "imperialistic" oppression. The charge of imperialism, which Communists continually use against Western nations, is grounded in the teaching of Lenin. His theory of imperialism was an attempt to explain why the conditions of the working class had not grown progressively worse under capitalism and why the capitalist system itself had not been overthrown as Marx and Engels had predicted.

Since the predictions of Marx and Engels had been disproved by the facts of history, it was necessary to introduce a new factor in an effort to account for their errors and, at the same time, one which could be explained as a logical extension of their basic theory. This new factor, according to Lenin, was imperialism.

Lenin distinguished between two stages in the development of capitalism. The first of these he called industrial capitalism, when capitalism was advancing, and the second, imperialism or monopoly capitalism, when capitalism was dying. Under industrial capitalism, Lenin theorized, power in society was in the hands of the factory owners. However, as a result of intense competition between capitalists, more and more of them were driven into the ranks of the working class. This led to the concentration of more and more capital in the hands of fewer and fewer capitalists. As a result, industrial monopolies developed in the form of huge corporations.

Lenin contended that, as a result of this new concentration of capital, a merger developed between industrial and banking interests which led to control of society by financiers. In other words, power in capitalist society had been transferred from the factory owners to the financiers. With this development, Lenin argued, competition between capitalists for export trade was replaced by competition between financiers to invest their surplus capital abroad and to locate and control more foreign markets.

Through the formation of international cartels, Lenin envisioned the division of the world into areas of economic and political domination. This domination, according to Lenin, would give rise to the era of imperialism, beyond which capitalism could develop no further. Moreover, while the division of territory might at first be amicable, it would, said Lenin, inevitably lead to war as imperialist nations expanded their colonial empires.

According to Lenin's theory of imperialism, the exploitation of colonial countries enabled the capitalists to grant some minor concessions to the working class of their own nations to lessen their oppression and to blunt temporarily their realization of the need to overthrow the capitalist system. However, the concessions to workers in industrial nations were granted at the expense of workers in colonial nations.

This theoretical development expanded the Communist concept of the working class to include the exploited masses of the colonial nations, as well as those of the industrially developed nations. Therefore, according to Lenin, every nation which was the subject of capitalist exploitation became a likely prospect for a successful Communist revolution.

Fallacies in Lenin's Theory

Just as history has disproved the theory of Marx and Engels, it has disproved Lenin's theory of imperialism. Many of the former colonial possessions of the highly industrialized nations have since gained, or are in the process of gaining, their independence. When the United Nations met in its first session in 1946, there were only 51 member nations. Membership has increased to more than a hundred, and the prospects are that the number will increase still further. The increase can be traced almost exclusively to the granting of independence to former colonial dependencies by the nations of the West.

Contrary to Lenin's analysis, the highly industrialized nations have become less and less dependent upon the underdeveloped countries for raw materials. Labor unions and farm organizations have developed as counter forces to what Lenin described as monopoly capitalism. Moreover, legislation in the form of antitrust statutes and tax regulations serves as an additional restraint. Subsequent economic developments illustrate that, contrary to Lenin's theory, the nations of the free world are voluntarily cooperating with one another. Since World War II, for example, there have been such measures as the Marshall Plan, the Point Four Program, the General Agreement on Tariffs and Trade, the European Common Market, the Alliance for Progress, and the Organization for Economic Cooperation and Development.

Communist Peace

We have seen how the Communists seized control of one country, Russia, and consolidated their hold on that country through the Communist party. We have seen how, in turn, the Communist system produced a dictator who, through his control of the party, controlled the country. We have seen how that country was used as the base for the extension of communism in other lands. According to Communist dogma, the expansion must continue by any and all means until the final goal of world communism has been achieved. Only then, the Communists claim, will true peace prevail throughout the world. What they actually mean is that peace will be achieved only when they have crushed all opposition and have succeeded in imposing their will on all the other countries of the world.

Chapter 10

Communism versus Nationalism

It is a basic tenet of communism that the establishment of a world-wide classless society will result in the elimination of conflicting views and jealousies based on national interest. From this, it naturally should follow that as the number of Communist countries increases, there should be a decrease in the conflicts of interest among them. This seemed to be the case during the first 30-year period of the existence and growth of the Communist empire. The Communist-bloc countries gave every appearance of having achieved a monolithic unity based on common interests.

Appearances, however, are sometimes deceptive. What appeared to be monolithic unity based on common interests was primarily a unity which resulted from the awesome authority of the Soviet Union as the first and, for some time, the only country in which Communists had seized power. Other factors which contributed to this apparent unity were the ruthless dictatorial power of Joseph Stalin within the international Communist movement, and the dependence of other communist parties on the obviously greater economic and military resources of the Soviet Union.

Soviet leadership of the international Communist movement was accepted unquestioningly by all other Communist parties until challenged by Yugoslavia in 1948. This was only one of a number of challenges, some of which took the form of armed uprisings, that were to develop with growing intensity as the national interests of the other countries in the Communist bloc clashed with the imperialistic designs of the Soviet Union.

Several other factors contributed to the growing clash of interests in the Communist camp after 1948. These included the conditions under which various Communist regimes had come to power, the death of Stalin in 1953 and the subsequent reappraisal of him by Khrushchev, and the Communist seizure of power in China, a nation with a population three times that of the Soviet Union which had imperialistic designs of its own. Because each Communist-bloc country has its own national interests based on distinguishable historical, cultural, ethnic, economic, and political backgrounds, each country's domestic and foreign policies often conflict with the national interests of the others, and disputes, contrary to Communist doctrine, are inevitable. *It is important to remember, however, that disputes among nations of the Communist bloc do not mean that they have abandoned their strategic goal of world-wide communism. They merely disagree on the tactics to be emphasized to achieve that objective.*

Yugoslavia

In 1948, Yugoslavia's Marshal Tito defied Stalin's absolute authority and control over the international Communist movement. It was an event which brought immediate repercussions in the Communist camp and one which was to create complex and perplexing problems on the international scene.

Josip Broz Tito was one of the early organizers of the Communist movement in Yugoslavia. When Yugoslavia, which had been invaded and overrun by Germany in April, 1941, formally surrendered on June 15, 1941, Tito and his Communist followers viewed the defeat as an opportunity for a Communist revolution.

Since Germany had defeated Yugoslavia while the Nazi-Soviet nonaggression pact was still in effect the Yugoslav Communists were faced with a dilemma. How could they revolt against the Nazi conquerors who were then allied with the Soviet Union? This dilemma was resolved for them a week later when, on June 22, Germany attacked the Soviet Union. On that day, Tito issued a proclamation that had been printed on secret presses and distributed hurriedly by couriers to all parts of Yugoslavia. It read, in part:

The hour has struck to take arms for your freedom against
Fascist aggressors. Do your part in the fight for freedom
under the leadership of the Communist Party of Yugoslavia. The war of the Soviet Union is your war, because
the Soviet Union is fighting against your enemies, under
whose yoke your necks are bent.

For the Yugoslav Communists, the so-called imperialist war had
been transformed into a revolutionary "war of national liberation." In the confusion and chaos that prevailed, the disciplined
and well-organized Communist forces emerged as the leaders of
the resistance movement against the Nazis. In March, 1945, Tito
became head of the government. The Yugoslav people had shed
the Nazi yoke, only to have it replaced with another.

After Tito's ascendancy to power, there was no law except
Communist law. Anti-Communist "enemies" were liquidated.
"People's courts" were formed and "people's judges" appointed
to dispense Communist "justice." A secret-police organization
launched a wave of terror. On his own scale, Tito emulated
Stalin in carrying out an extensive program of regimentation of
daily life in Yugoslavia. Yugoslav Communists followed Moscow's
direction without question, actually looking forward to the time
that their country would become a constituent part of the Soviet
Union.

The Cominform

Yugoslavia's strategic location in Europe and the stature of the
Yugoslav party as compared to the parties in the other satellite
nations were probably responsible for the Soviet decision to establish the headquarters of a new international Communist organization in Belgrade. After the dissolution of the Comintern
in 1943, the world Communist movement had no formal organization. The need for such an organization became apparent when
problems arose among different Communist parties following
World War II. Typical of these were the dispute between the
parties of Yugoslavia and Italy over the disposition of Trieste and
the original intention of Poland and Czechoslovakia to participate
in the Marshall Plan. The new organization was called the Information Bureau of the Communist and Workers' Parties, or as
it is generally known, the Cominform. Membership in the Cominform was limited to the Communist parties of the Soviet Union,

Yugoslavia, Poland, Bulgaria, Rumania, Hungary, Czechoslovakia, France, and Italy.

Because Tito and his Yugoslav Communists were regarded as faithful supporters of the Soviet Union, it came as a surprise when, in 1948, the Yugoslav party was expelled from the Cominform. Headquarters for the Cominform were transferred from Belgrade to Bucharest, Rumania. Yugoslavia then became the target for intensive economic and political pressure directed by Moscow in an attempt to force Tito to submit to Soviet control.

Various factors contributed to Tito's refusal to submit to Soviet control. Certainly an important one was the fact that the Yugoslav Communists had come to power with comparatively little assistance from the Soviet Army. They were proud of their accomplishment, but the Soviet Union belittled it and expected the same subservience that it demanded of its other satellites. There is evidence, too, that the Red Army, during the period that it was in Yugoslavia toward the end of World War II, was guilty of widespread atrocities and plunder. There were other factors, but in the final analysis the most important reason was Tito's refusal to accept the principle that the interests of the world Communist movement necessarily coincided with Soviet national interests.

After 1948, Tito was to pursue a course which he described as "national communism." This doctrine holds that each nation can find its own way to communism without slavishly following the example of the Soviet Union. However, it does not constitute a rejection of the principles of Marxism-Leninism.

East Germany

In June, 1953, a riot broke out in East Berlin. There, rebelling against the suppression of religious freedom, the shortage of food, and an increase in production quotas, workers seized the factories. Riots spread quickly throughout the Soviet zone in East Germany and threatened to topple the Communist regime. The ranks of the rioters grew to an estimated total of 200,000 workers. Among them were many Vopos, the Communist police, who joined their countrymen in defiance of the Communist regime and added their guns to the limited arms available to the rioters.

On June 17, 1953, the day after the rioting began, Soviet tanks and soldiers were sent to meet the challenge to Communist authority. The crowd was no match for the Soviet troops and their weapons. Despite the uneven nature of the struggle, however, they tried to pit their physical strength against the tanks. The extent of their gallant but futile efforts was measurable by the number of dead bodies lying in the streets by nightfall. The uprising had been quelled, and Soviet authority was re-established. A reshuffling of personnel led to the emergence of the Soviet puppet Walter Ulbricht as head of Communist East Germany. It was not the last time, however, that Communist authority was to be challenged in such fashion, nor the last time that ruthless Communist leadership was to be maintained in the same manner that it originally had been gained—through the might of the Red Army.

Poland

Three years later, demonstrations erupted in Poznan, Poland. In June, 1956, workers there staged a general strike. Several thousand people marched and demanded freedom, bread, and the departure of the Russians. Riots ensued and were met by army tanks. More than 50 people were killed and some 200 were wounded. Moscow attributed the riots to "foreign imperialist" agents who were attempting to weaken the so-called Socialist countries. However, Communist officials in Poland subsequently exposed Moscow's claim as propaganda by admitting that there was intense dissatisfaction among the Polish people.

Although the rioting was suppressed, the dissatisfaction did not subside. Another flare-up occurred in October, 1956, when Khrushchev and other Soviet officials appeared in Warsaw unexpectedly while a new Politburo of the Polish Communist party was being selected. The arrival of the Soviet officials was accompanied by movements of Soviet Army units toward Warsaw and of a Soviet naval squadron toward Gdansk.

All factions in the Polish Communist party wanted Wladyslaw Gomulka as leader. Gomulka, however, insisted on the dismissal of all Stalinists from key positions and, in a stormy meeting with the Soviet leaders, convinced them that Poland had to pursue a more independent course toward communism. In presenting his problem to the people, Gomulka emphasized that there were many roads to socialism and that future relations between the Soviet Union and Poland would have to be based on a greater degree of independence and equality.

In the face of demonstrations by the Polish people in support of Gomulka, Soviet leaders, who were originally opposed to him, acquiesced and returned to Moscow. Shortly thereafter, the Soviet "maneuvers" ended.

Moscow's gamble on Gomulka paid off. Within a year, he was to demonstrate his reliance on the use of force and violence to maintain communism's hold on the Polish people. For a short time after gaining power in October, 1956, he permitted some cultural and political freedom in Poland. He managed to keep the seething dissatisfaction of the people in check by warning that the Russians might intervene if Polish demands for independence from Moscow became too strong.

In August, 1957, Gomulka demonstrated his willingness to rule through force. When streetcar and bus workers instituted a strike to protest their poor living conditions and low wages, Gomulka ordered it smashed by armed troops and the use of tear gas. In October, 1957, a newspaper critical of Gomulka's policies was closed down. When the ban was followed by student riots, Gomulka again used troops and tear gas to smash the opposition. This was followed by a law that writers must write in accordance with the policies of the Polish Communist party.

By the end of his first year in power, Gomulka had left no doubt of his link to Moscow. He stated, "I realize very well where the future of the Polish nation and of the Polish working class lies," and added unequivocally, "it is not with the West."

Hungary

Another explosion in a Soviet-satellite nation presented a greater problem for the Kremlin. Its solution to that problem reverberated throughout the world. Possibly inspired by the events in Poland, the people of Hungary arose in open revolt on October 23, 1956, just two days after Gomulka's election in Poland. Earlier, in June, Hungarian workers had heard of and expressed their sympathy for the Polish workers' strikes and demonstrations in Poznan. In addition, Hungary had been undergoing a de-Stalinization campaign which had resulted in the exposure of many of the injustices prevalent in Hungary under the Communist regime.

Students at Budapest University started the uprising on October 23, 1956, with a demonstration, demanding the return of full national independence. Events moved swiftly. Workers joined the movement, and statues of Stalin and other symbols of Soviet domination of Hungary were destroyed. Hungarian armed forces joined their fellow citizens in the revolt, and within five days Hungary was almost free of Soviet control, despite the intervention of some Soviet troops. Imre Nagy became the prime minister of Hungary. On November 1, 1956, he declared Hungary a neutral nation and announced its intention to withdraw from the Warsaw Pact.

Although the fighting had ceased, the Soviets moved additional troops into Hungary. At the same time, they requested negotiations, allegedly to discuss the manner in which Soviet troops were to be withdrawn. Then they arrested the Hungarian negotiators and replaced Nagy with Janos Kadar, while Soviet troops crushed the rebellion. Hungary suffered over 25,000 casualties, and more than 100,000 Hungarians fled to the West. Once again, the Soviet Army had played its role in maintaining communism's slave empire.

When Prime Minister Imre Nagy was deposed by the Soviets, he fled to the sanctuary of the Yugoslav embassy in Budapest. At the time, he was one of the most sought-after men in Hungary. The freedom-fighters wanted him restored as prime minister. The new Soviet puppet-ruler, Janos Kadar, wanted to use him politically to appease the freedom-fighters. The Russians simply wanted him.

Nagy emerged from the Yugoslav embassy after 19 days of sanctuary there. He did so because the Kadar regime gave the Yugoslavs a written guarantee that Nagy and his associates would not be molested. Following their appearance into the open, Nagy and his colleagues were seized by the Russians as they started for their homes. The tragic climax to this violation of agreement was revealed in June, 1958, with the announcement by Moscow that Nagy and some of his associates had been executed after having been tried secretly.

Dissolution of the Cominform

The treacherous attack on Hungary by the Soviet Union climaxed a year of ferment within the Communist camp. Khrushchev had caused much of the ferment by starting the de-Stalinization campaign with his secret speech at the Twentieth Congress of the Communist Party of the Soviet Union in February, 1956. The East European satellite countries had followed his lead in exposing and examining the "mistakes and shortcomings" of their respective governments and in exonerating former leaders who had been deposed earlier.

An anticlimax to the events of 1956 in the Communist camp was a renewed Soviet attack on Tito. It marked the end of an extensive campaign which Khrushchev had conducted after Stalin's death to bring Tito back into the fold. The highlights of the campaign included Khrushchev's assertion that there were many roads to socialism, which was an obvious concession to Tito, and, even more important, the dissolution of the Cominform. On April 17, 1956, the Cominform was dissolved as an obvious gesture toward reconciliation with Tito.

The dissolution of the Cominform showed the emphasis which Khrushchev had placed on the campaign to establish better relations with Tito. The importance of the campaign was also shown by Khrushchev's reference to Tito in the secret speech exposing Stalin's crimes. Khrushchev said: "I recall the first days when the conflict between the Soviet Union and Yugoslavia began artificially to be blown up." He reported that Stalin had once declared: "I will shake my little finger—and there will be no more Tito. He will fall." Then Khrushchev went on to say: "But this did not happen to Tito." He concluded with the observation:

> We have carefully examined the case of Yugoslavia and have found a proper solution which is approved by the peoples of the Soviet Union and of Yugoslavia as well as by the working masses of all the people's democracies and by all progressive humanity. The liquidation of the abnormal relationship with Yugoslavia was done in the interest of the whole camp of Socialism, in the interest of strengthening peace in the whole world.

National Communism Rejected

The "liquidation of the abnormal relationship" claim of Khrushchev appeared to have been borne out when the signing of a Soviet-Yugoslav pact was announced in June, 1956. The pact was signed as a joint declaration of renewed relations between their respective countries and acknowledged that the conditions for achieving communism vary in different countries. They pledged future cooperation between their countries based on a spirit of freedom and equality. The agreement condemned any efforts of one country in the Communist bloc to impose its views on another country in the bloc. In addition, the agreement called for the free and comradely exchange of experiences and views and outlined a plan for maintaining relations through personal contacts, exchanges of delegations, and joint meetings of party workers.

However, after the brutal onslaught on Hungary by Soviet tanks and troops, Yugoslav Communists criticized the Soviet intervention. Yugoslav Vice President Edvard Kardelj, speaking in the Yugoslav Parliament in December, 1956, described the Hungarian revolt as a rebellion of the working class against an intolerable system in which there was no democracy. Kardelj indicated that the Soviet Union had erred in its intervention in Hungary. The Soviet answer came in the form of a year-end interview of Khrushchev on December 31, 1956, reported in a Czechoslovak Communist newspaper. Khrushchev declared that national communism was invalid and was injurious to the whole family of Socialist nations.

But even Khrushchev could not stamp out the "disease" of national communism or the tendency of some other leaders of Communist-bloc countries to question whether the interests of the international Communist movement necessarily coincide with the interests of the Soviet Union.

Effect of Soviet Scientific Advances

The scientific and technological successes of the Soviet Union in 1957 did much to solidify its position of leadership among the Communist-bloc countries. The Soviet Union drew world-wide attention with its achievements in the military-scientific sphere, notably the launching of two earth satellites and the development of advanced types of aircraft and intercontinental ballistic missiles. The Soviet Union used the accomplishments not only to impress the West with its increased military capabilities, but also to enhance its stature within the Communist bloc.

These accomplishments had a noticeable impact on the leaders of other Communist-bloc countries. For example, in November, 1957, while attending the Moscow celebration of the fortieth anniversary of the Bolshevik revolution, both Mao Tse-tung and

Gomulka led a host of visiting Communists in acknowledging Soviet leadership in the world Communist movement.

Mao's ostensible acceptance of Soviet leadership in 1957 was soon to be contradicted by growing evidence of Chinese Communist differences with Moscow. China's economic dependence upon the Soviet Union was balanced by the fact that the Chinese Communists, like the Yugoslavs, had won power more or less on their own. Moreover, Chinese Communists are unwilling to concede the pre-eminence of Khrushchev over Mao as the interpreter of Marxism-Leninism. While the Red Chinese adhere to the basic goal of world-wide communism, they differ greatly with Khrushchev regarding the means by which Communist domination is to be achieved.

Peaceful Coexistence

Soviet leaders are faced with the need to consolidate territorial and economic gains made during World War II and immediately thereafter. They must also attempt to thwart such free-world alliances as the North Atlantic Treaty Organization and the Southeast Asia Treaty Organization designed to oppose further Communist aggression. In addition, they undoubtedly realize the consequences of an all-out nuclear war. These factors demanded the development of a strategy short of full-scale nuclear warfare. Key to the new Soviet strategy is the so-called *peaceful coexistence* policy. It is a broad, psychological tactic cleverly devised by Khrushchev to serve a number of objectives. It is another powerful weapon in the Communist arsenal of deception, a weapon concealed behind an alluring campaign designed to provide a cover for the goal of attaining a world-wide Communist society through revolutionary means.

Through the weapon of peaceful coexistence, Soviet Communists are seeking to lull the free world—particularly the United States—into a false sense of security. It is a means of buying time through which they can consolidate past gains while probing for soft spots in the non-Communist world which present opportunities for future expansion.

Khrushchev's policy of peaceful coexistence is not based on weakness. On the contrary, it is an indication of strength and confidence. Taking cognizance of the gains made by communism during and after World War II and stimulated by Soviet scientific successes and demonstrated military might, Khrushchev has discarded Stalin's old theory of the threat of "capitalist encirclement." He has replaced it with the theory that the world balance of power has shifted in favor of the Communist-bloc countries to such a degree that war between capitalism and communism is no longer fatalistically inevitable.

Lenin had declared that war between capitalism and communism was inevitable—that eventually there must be a clash between the two systems. Khrushchev explains his modification of Lenin's theory by stating that Lenin was correct in the light of circumstances in his time, but changing conditions have altered the world balance of power in favor of communism.

Peaceful coexistence is the ideological crux of the dispute between the Soviets and the Chinese Communists, because the latter still hold to Lenin's theory of the inevitability of war. But again, as is the case in most Communist disputes, the ideological argument serves only as a cover for underlying differences.

Sino-Soviet Dispute

For example, one of the major factors underlying the dispute between the Soviet Union and Communist China is that they are in different stages of development. Consequently, theories and programs designed for the domestic and foreign affairs of the one often conflict with the national interests of the other. This is particularly true of both the de-Stalinization campaign and the tactic of peaceful coexistence. The de-Stalinization campaign has been of very practical value to Soviet Communists in that it provided a scapegoat for past "mistakes" and facilitated the transition of power into Khrushchev's hands while avoiding a major upheaval internally.

But Chinese Communist leaders feel that the present stage of economic development in their country compels them to use the oppressive measures usually associated with Stalin in collectivizing and industrializing their country. Moreover, Mao Tse-tung has been made a demigod in Red China, just as Stalin was in the Soviet Union. Therefore, Soviet criticism of the "cult of the personality" could be interpreted as indirect criticism of Mao.

During 1958, Mao Tse-tung announced a program designed to enable China to make a "great leap forward." A major feature of the program was the establishment of a commune system. The communes regimented China's labor force into semi-military groups in order to increase China's industrial capacity. The Chinese claimed that through the communes they had found a short cut to communism. To the Soviets, who ridiculed the claim, it represented an implied challenge to their self-assigned role as the most authoritative interpreters of Marxist-Leninist concepts.

The "great leap forward" was supposed to transform Communist China rapidly from an agricultural country to a major industrial power. The immediate goal was to rival Great Britain, and ultimately the United States. While dependent upon the Soviet Union for economic and technical assistance, Communist China aimed to accomplish its objective largely through the exploitation of the one resource it had in a quantity which no other nation could match—its vast population.

The Chinese Communists are trying to drive the people to unrealistic goals by inhuman demands for greater and greater personal sacrifice. Red China hopes to accomplish its objectives by constant propagandizing of the long-suffering people and threatening them with the "dangers of American imperialism." The creation of hate for a contrived external enemy has long been the psychological conditioning practiced by dictators to spur their subjects to still greater sacrifices.

The regimentation, the famines, and the attempts to accomplish too much too quickly threw the entire economy of China into chaos. The "great leap forward" became a great leap to catastrophe. Not only did Communist China fail to achieve its immediate goal of rivalling Great Britain, it also failed to achieve even a minimum standard of economic balance. It created such a serious disruption of the economy that the Communist leaders of the country had to go outside of the Communist nations—to Australia, France, and Canada—to purchase more than $350,-000,000 worth of food.

In the drive for rapid industrialization, Chinese Communist leaders are not motivated by a desire to improve the lot of the Chinese people, but rather by a desire to build the country into a militant world power. They hope to build a nation which, supported by military and economic might, can compete with the great powers in influencing the course of history.

The compulsion of Chinese Communist leaders to transform China into a great power is not confined to domestic matters. Just as the Soviet Union expanded its empire by aggression in Europe, Chinese Communists look toward expansion throughout

Asia. In connection with this desire, they have conquered and ruthlessly suppressed the inhabitants of Tibet and annexed disputed territory also claimed by India. They have sent "volunteers" to fight in Korea and have given military support to Communist guerrilla fighters in countries such as South Vietnam and Laos. Throughout Southeast Asia, they solicit support of their revolutionary activities from among the millions of overseas Chinese residing in the area. All of this is part of the Chinese Communist design to create an empire in Asia.

The tactic of peaceful coexistence is of practical value to the Soviet Union in the field of international relations in providing them with an element essential to their aims—time. But Chinese Communist leaders feel that peaceful coexistence curbs the revolutionary ardor through which they hope to achieve their own imperialistic goals. They continue to promote the idea that war is inevitable and that militant revolutionary activity is vital for further expansion of communism.

In the past few years, both the Soviet Union and Communist China have engaged in increasing criticism of each other's views. The Soviets contend that the Chinese Communists are "dogmatists," charging that they fail to interpret and apply Marxism-Leninism in the light of changing conditions. The Chinese Communists retaliate with charges that the Soviets are "revisionists," who are guilty of unwarranted deviations from basic principles of Marxism-Leninism. They insist that the policy of peaceful coexistence is impeding the class struggle in the capitalist nations and is detrimental to the promotion of "wars of liberation" in the underdeveloped countries. Thus, by encouraging militancy on the part of the Communist parties in underdeveloped countries, the Chinese Communists are attempting to assert their leadership in the international Communist movement.

During 1960, Albania joined Communist China in questioning the validity of Soviet policies. Like their counterparts in Yugoslavia and China, Albanian Communists owed little to the Soviet Union in connection with their seizure of power in the tiny country. However, the Albanian Communists did receive support from the Yugoslav Communists and have long feared that Tito might seize upon this as the basis for the annexation of Albania. They suspected that a reconciliation between the Soviet Union and Yugoslavia might be made at their expense. In addition, they look favorably on Communist China because it furnished them much-needed grain at a time when it could ill afford to do so.

Thus, the international Communist movement is marked by a variety of disputes. They all serve to illustrate what Communist ideology denies—that there can be conflicting views and jealousies among Communist countries based on national interests. But the fact that the disputes exist offers little comfort to the free world. This is so because the dispute between the Soviet Union and Communist China is not over the strategic goal, which is the domination of the world, but merely over the tactics to be emphasized to achieve that goal.

Part Five

Challenge to Freedom

Chapter 11

Communism's Target—
the United States

The United States is the major target for attack by the forces of the world Communist movement. This is not a figment of the imagination. It is a hard, realistic statement of purpose which was the essence of a Communist declaration to the world in 1960.

In November, 1960, representatives of 81 Communist parties convened in Moscow. After extended discussions, they unanimously adopted and issued a lengthy statement that well might be termed a new *Communist Manifesto*. It paid lip service to the unity of the Communist countries under the leadership of the Soviet Union and reiterated the determination of the world Communist movement to achieve the goal of world domination.

In that Communist declaration of purpose, the United States was singled out as the main enemy of communism. Communists throughout the world were called upon to use any and all means to disrupt and weaken the influence and strength of the United States, the principal deterrent to further Communist expansion.

A particularly vital element of the over-all Communist strategy for attacking the United States in full force has since become apparent. It is the intensification of Communist activities within the United States.

Representatives of the Communist Party of the United States attended the Moscow conference in 1960. The Communist Party, USA, following its historical pattern of undeviating support of the Soviet Union responded to the call for a stepped-up attack on this country by intensifying its efforts to penetrate and exploit all areas of our society.

Communist-bloc agents in the United States increased their clandestine efforts as part of a build-up of spying operations throughout the world. The relentless quest for information by Communist spies in the United States constitutes the most massive offensive of its type ever conducted by one nation against another in the history of international relations. The Soviet Union directs, controls, and coordinates Communist subversive and clandestine activities aimed at destroying the internal security of the United States.

The massive Communist offensive directed at the free world in general and the United States in particular clearly exposes the false nature of the tactic of peaceful coexistence. The preservation of the American way of life and the establishment of true world peace are goals endangered by the enormity of the present Communist challenge to free men everywhere.

Since its inception, the Communist Party, USA, has been unswerving in its allegiance to the Soviet Union, which is committed to the goal of world domination by communism. Because the United States is the principal deterrent to further Communist expansion, the Communist Party, USA, is, and will continue to be, a serious threat to our internal security.

Khrushchev's Visits to the United States

Many people throughout the world have been inclined to look upon Nikita S. Khrushchev as a new and less menacing Communist leader. Various factors have contributed to the acceptance of this belief, including the de-Stalinization campaign and Khrushchev's policy of peaceful coexistence.

The world has been subjected to an intense propaganda barrage concerning peaceful coexistence. Khrushchev gave the people of the United States a firsthand opportunity to view the originator and manipulator of the campaign when he visited this country in 1959.

It was a visit that Americans will not soon forget. Khrushchev used all the tactics characteristic of the Soviet Union's effort to sell peaceful coexistence to the world. On September 27, 1959, the curtain came down on Khrushchev's one-man show. His farewell television address that evening tied together the loose ends of his theme of peaceful coexistence that he had unwound across the nation during his two-week visit.

Khrushchev's television message to the American people that evening was the most dramatic propaganda appeal of his entire visit. This was Khrushchev at his artful best. Gone were the angry gestures, the vulgarities, the bombast, and the bluster which had marked some of his other appearances throughout the tour. Khrushchev tried to erase the image of the bold, brash, challenging, and threatening figure who had monopolized the news during the previous two weeks and substituted the image of a gentle, kindly, peace-loving man.

Khrushchev's speech was a skillful blend of half-truth and fancy. He touched only briefly on some of the major issues—the cold war, disarmament, and Germany. He completely ignored others. Instead, he presented a bright picture of life under communism—allegedly the most humane political, social, and economic system ever devised by man. Khrushchev implied that there was only one thing lacking to make the picture perfect—world peace, but on Communist terms. With world peace, the money now being spent on armaments could be diverted toward making life better for both American and Soviet peoples.

The "New Communist Manifesto"

For those both in this country and elsewhere who may have succumbed to the lure of Khrushchev's performance, the year 1960 drew to a close on two notes of special significance that should have dispelled all doubts about Khrushchev's true intentions. The first was Khrushchev's contemptuous, shoe-pounding display of unbridled, dictatorial arrogance at the Fifteenth General Assembly of the United Nations at New York City in October, 1960. Of still greater importance was the meeting of representatives of 81 Communist parties from throughout the world that convened in Moscow in November, 1960. The delegates to that meeting formulated a document of intentions which should have served to alert all free nations everywhere to the growing threat which communism represents to freedom.

Issued in December, 1960, the document constituted, in effect, a new Communist manifesto. Hidden among the semantic distortions in the new Communist manifesto was the declaration of purpose. Divested of all semantic subterfuge, the purpose emerged as a clear and unequivocal call for the launching of a new and all-out offensive by Communists everywhere in support of the program for world conquest.

Of utmost importance in the new manifesto was its singling out of the United States as the main enemy. The United States was attacked as "the mainstay of colonialism today" and branded as "the main economic, financial and military force of modern imperialism."

The Moscow declaration of 1960 amounted to an unmistakable call for an attack on all human freedoms and non-Communist governments through widespread infiltration and subversion of non-Communist groups and intensified agitation of the so-called class struggle. The declaration contained the statement that "it is of the utmost importance that Communists should extend their work in trade unions and cooperatives, among the peasantry, the youth, the women, in sports organizations, and the unorganized sections of the population."

Not to be overlooked in the Communist call to action was the emphasis on youth. "There are new opportunities now to draw the younger generation into the struggle for peace and democracy, and for the great ideals of communism," the manifesto read, adding that "Lenin's great behest—to go deeper into the masses, to work wherever there are masses, to strengthen the ties with the masses in order to lead them—must become a major task for every Communist party."

Soviet Influence

Representatives of the Communist Party, USA, participated with the representatives of other Communist parties in the Moscow conference. While the party did not, for tactical reasons, formally adopt the 81-party statement which was issued on December 5, 1960, the Communist Party, USA, by its participation in the conference once again demonstrated that it acknowledges the leadership of the Communist Party of the Soviet Union. The entire history of the Communist Party, USA, demonstrates conclusively that it has selected its leaders, formulated its policies, and shifted its tactics, either on the basis of specific Soviet directives, or as a reflex response to Soviet action. To this day, the Communists in the United States pledge their allegiance to the Soviet Union.

As previously shown, the concept of democratic centralism provides the means for Communist party leaders to keep a firm hand on the reins to guide party activities. By controlling the leaders of the majority of the Communist parties throughout the world, the Soviets are able to control the activities of those parties. This control is based on the acknowledgment of dependence upon the Soviets by the various parties for both material support and ideological leadership, and it is exercised by the Soviets' approval or disapproval of the policies being followed by the leadership of individual parties.

Expulsion of Browder

It will be recalled, for example, that the Soviets used effective means to replace Jay Lovestone as the leading figure of the Communist Party, USA, in 1929 to insure that the Communist leadership here obeyed Stalin's dictates. A similar example occurred in 1945 and resulted in the ouster of Earl Browder as leader of the Communist Party, USA.

In 1944, on the recommendation of Browder, who was then general secretary, the Communist Party, USA, had changed its name to the "Communist Political Association" in line with Soviet efforts during that period to enlist all possible support from the United States in the war against Germany. However, Browder erred in assuming that the Soviet Union's desire for wartime cooperation with its allies was to be followed by an extended postwar period of international cooperation.

The Soviet Union had planned an entirely different course of action. With its safety assured, the Soviet Union had no further need for an alliance with the United States. To Stalin, the time had come to press forward again with Communist designs. In 1945, the Communist Party of the Soviet Union ordered the reconstitution of the Communist party in this country as a militant, Marxist-Leninist organization.

The reconstitution of the Communist Party, USA, was ordered through an article written by the French Communist leader Jacques Duclos shortly after returning to France from Moscow.

This article severely criticized Browder, characterized the wartime dissolution of the Communist Party, USA, as an unwarranted revision of Marxism-Leninism, and called on Communists in the United States to reconsider their action. Dutifully admitting their error, the leaders of the party, at a special convention in July, 1945, reconstituted the Communist Party, USA. With Moscow's blessing William Z. Foster assumed the leadership of the Communist movement in the United States. In February, 1946, Browder was expelled from the party for his deviation.

Factional Struggle

Soviet influence over the leadership of the party was again demonstrated in 1956 and 1957. The downgrading of Stalin by Khrushchev, evidences of anti-Semitism in Communist nations, and the intervention of Soviet troops in the Hungarian revolt led to dissension in the leadership of the Communist Party, USA. A group, led by John Gates, criticized Foster's leadership and advocated the transformation of the party into a political-action association which could formulate its policies without blindly following the dictates of the Soviet Union.

The Communist Party of the Soviet Union used several methods to insure that the party would not fall into the hands of Gates and that it would continue to be an arm of Soviet policy. A September, 1956, article in *Pravda,* organ of the Central Committee of the Communist Party of the Soviet Union, for example, praised Foster as a "noted theoretician and Marxist historian," devoted to the struggle for doctrinal purity and unity of the Communist Party, USA, against what were called opportunists and diversionists. The proposal of Gates to transform the party into a political-action association was defeated overwhelmingly at the party's Sixteenth National Convention in February, 1957. Belatedly seeing the handwriting on the Kremlin wall, Gates finally resigned from the Party in January, 1958.

New Leadership

In December, 1959, soon after Khrushchev's visit, the Communist Party, USA, elected Moscow-trained Gus Hall as its new general secretary at the Seventeenth National Convention. Moscow's control over the Communist Party, USA, is symbolized by Hall, whose parents were charter members of the party. Having joined the party in 1927, Hall went to the Soviet Union in 1931 to attend the Lenin School, where students were trained in the tactics of revolution and civil war, as well as in sabotage and guerrilla warfare.

As previously noted, Hall upon his return to the United States, testified in 1934 that he would "prefer America with a Soviet government" and when asked, "And you are willing to fight and overthrow this government?" he answered, "Absolutely." When asked, "And you are willing to take up arms and overthrow the constituted authorities?" Hall answered, "When the time comes, yes."

Undeviating Loyalty to Soviet Union

That the Communist Party of the Soviet Union has been able to guide party activities through control of the leadership is evidenced by the fact that the Communist Party, USA, has never failed to change its line to conform with instructions from or developments within the Soviet Union, even though, at times, this has meant a complete reversal of policy. For example, after the signing of the nonaggression pact which made the Soviet Union and Nazi Germany allies, the Communist Party, USA, dropped its militant fight against fascism, and its attempts to justify Soviet action in signing a pact with the hated Nazi regime caused a sizable drop in membership.

At the outbreak of World War II when the Soviet Union was allied with Germany, the party labeled the conflict an "imperialist war" in which the United States had no legitimate interest. Communists in the United States opposed military conscription, formed peace mobilization fronts and anti-imperialist leagues, and coined the slogan, "The Yanks Are Not Coming."

When, on June 22, 1941, the Nazi-Soviet alliance was shattered by the German attack on the Soviet Union, the so-called "imperialist war" was magically transformed by Communist jargon into a "just" war and a "war of liberation." The peace mobilization fronts and anti-imperialist leagues of the Communist Party, USA, vanished into thin air, and the Communists changed their slogan to "The Yanks Are Not Coming Too Late!"

In support of Soviet policy after World War II, the Communist Party, USA, has made every effort to obstruct all measures which our nation has taken with the intention of defending itself and strengthening its allies against the threat of further Communist aggression. Among the measures which the party has opposed are the Marshall Plan, aid to Greece and Turkey, United Nations intervention in Korea and in the Congo, and the military, economic, and political agreements which the United States has made with other non-Communist nations throughout the world.

While opposing these measures, the party has consistently defended such acts of Communist aggression as the take-over in China and the brutal suppression of the uprisings in East Germany and Hungary. How unquestioning support of the Soviet Union can bring about a complete reversal of policy was again illustrated in 1961 when Khrushchev announced that the Soviet Union was resuming nuclear tests in the atmosphere and the United States announced on September 1 that the Soviet Union had fired the first bomb following Khrushchev's statement.

The announcement of the Soviet resumption of nuclear testing caused a hurried change in Communist propaganda tactics in this country and caught the party in an embarrassing situation. Just prior to the announcement, the September 3, 1961, issue of the east coast Communist newspaper, *The Worker,* had been printed and distributed by the thousands. Printed in advance of its publication date, this issue contained an editorial demand for "a permanent ban on testing." Thus, Communists here found themselves in the embarrassing position of appearing to be insisting on their demand two days after the Soviet Union had exploded a thermonuclear bomb.

Hasty action was called for to rectify the party's public position which was inconsistent with Moscow's action. The following issue of *The Worker,* dated September 10, 1961, proved the party's loyalty to Moscow and demonstrated the real hypocrisy of its earlier propaganda demand by featuring four articles on the first two pages attempting to explain, rationalize, and justify Soviet resumption of the nuclear tests.

The Communist Party, USA, has consistently avoided criticism of the Soviet Union or its leaders. Khrushchev's boorish behavior at the United Nations in 1960, was ignored by Communist publications in this country. Instead, the party saluted his "brilliant leadership" and praised him for his contributions to Marxism-Leninism.

To the leaders of the Communist movement in the United

States, the Khrushchev visits here in 1959 and 1960 served a valuable purpose. They used the visits to make optimistic predictions about the inevitable triumph of communism over capitalism. These predictions were uttered for a specific purpose, and not merely as idle boasts. The leaders of the party used the predictions to renew the loyalty and enthusiasm of its members and to spur them to even greater efforts in support of Communist causes. It was particularly important for them to inject new fervor into the Party members, because the party had been undergoing trying times.

Troubled Times

Over the years, widespread exposure of the party's essentially subversive nature and goals has helped to alert the American public to the threat which it represents. From 1951 to 1955, the party operated largely underground to hamper prosecution of its leaders by the government under the Smith Act, which prohibits advocacy of the violent overthrow of the government. But at the same time such hidden activities placed a heavy burden on its leadership as well as on the party's financial resources. Open party activity obviously is easier to direct and control than underground operations. The ordinary problems of coordinating a nationwide organization's activities are multiplied tenfold by the necessity for the relocation of personnel, the establishment of new lines of communication, the addition of extra security precautions, and similar measures which underground operations involve. It had been a difficult period for the party in this country.

The various government loyalty-security programs demanded by an aroused public opinion have been most effective in countering Communist attempts to infiltrate sensitive positions in government and industry. Of utmost importance is the fact that these measures have been accomplished within the framework of the traditional constitutional precepts of American justice.

Complicating the party's internal difficulties were international events bearing on the party's interests. The exposure of Stalin's totally corrupt practices by Khrushchev in 1956, the revelations of anti-Semitism in the Soviet Union, and the brutal aggression of the Soviet Union in crushing the Hungarian uprising, all contributed to disillusionment on the part of some party members.

This combination of national and international events caused a loss in party membership among the less dedicated of its adherents. The strongly disciplined, hard-core members were not shaken, however, and carried on their activities faithfully. Too, it should be noted that many of those who left the party during the difficult days did so only because of individual disagreement with leadership policies or tactics and not because of a rejection of Marxist-Leninist principles. Given different leadership, a shift of party tactics, or a popular issue for exploitation, they could be expected to resume their former party work and support. It was with such thoughts in mind that party leaders exploited the Khrushchev visits to this country in 1959–60, and sought to encourage many of the former party members to return to the fold.

Current Status of the Party

The Communist Party, USA, remains an integral part of the international Communist movement and remains dedicated to the goal of that movement—world conquest. In 1962, spokesmen for the party placed its membership at approximately 10,000. But, the actual strength and influence of the party cannot be measured solely in terms of numerical membership. As part of a movement which, in the comparatively short period of 45 years, has taken control of one-fourth of the world's territory and one-third of the world's population, and as part of a movement which has the backing of the military, scientific, industrial, and technological strength of the Soviet Union, the Communist Party, USA, is a serious threat as a fifth column within our borders.

Prior to his trip to the Soviet Union in January, 1961, press representatives asked the late William Z. Foster to comment on the strength of the party. Foster was quoted as saying that the Communist party in America was "potentially stronger than ever" and had "great opportunities before it." In February, 1962, Benjamin J. Davis, Jr., another veteran Communist in the United States, said: "I think the Communist party in America today is potentially the largest of all the political parties . . . some day in the future our party will be the most decisive party in the country." Of course, the opinions of Foster and Davis were based on the fact that the party is a part of the international Communist movement and their beliefs that the balance of forces in the world is shifting in favor of communism and that the complete triumph of communism is historically inevitable.

TYPICAL ORGANIZATION
OF COMMUNIST PARTY, USA

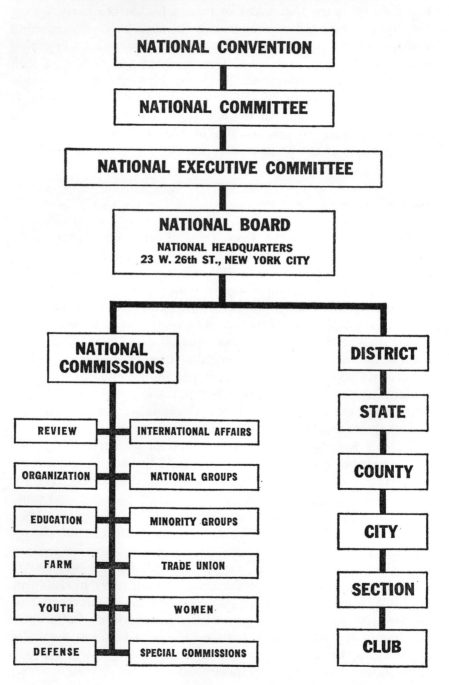

NATIONAL CONVENTION

NATIONAL COMMITTEE

NATIONAL EXECUTIVE COMMITTEE

NATIONAL BOARD
NATIONAL HEADQUARTERS
23 W. 26th ST., NEW YORK CITY

NATIONAL COMMISSIONS

REVIEW | INTERNATIONAL AFFAIRS
ORGANIZATION | NATIONAL GROUPS
EDUCATION | MINORITY GROUPS
FARM | TRADE UNION
YOUTH | WOMEN
DEFENSE | SPECIAL COMMISSIONS

DISTRICT

STATE

COUNTY

CITY

SECTION

CLUB

Khrushchev, in his opening address to the Twenty-second Congress of the Communist Party of the Soviet Union, referred to the Communist Party, USA, in these words: "The nugget is small, but its value is great." To fully comprehend the significance of Khrushchev's description, it is necessary only to contemplate the potential of 10,000 American supporters, backed by the United States, engaged in activities in the Soviet Union designed to overthrow its government.

Expanding Party Influence

The Communist Party, USA, realizes that if it is to accomplish its historic role it must constantly train new leadership and indoctrinate the membership in Marxism-Leninism. In furthering the Marxist education of its members, the party is stressing the study of the manual, *Fundamentals of Marxism-Leninism,* published by the Foreign Languages Publishing House in Moscow. Communist statements for public consumption to the contrary, the material furnished for study within the party clearly reveals that the use of force and violence is—as it has always been—the technique for the Communist seizure of power. For, *Fundamentals of Marxism-Leninism* specifically states: "The highest stage of the proletariat's class struggle is revolution."

As a minority group in the United States, the Communist party must also extend its influence above and beyond its own membership. As a highly disciplined and inherently conspiratorial group, the party achieves this goal through a variety of means. These include such tactics as propaganda; demonstrations; appeals for sympathy; operating through front groups; infiltrating and gaining control of non-Communist organizations, with special emphasis on labor unions and youth groups; maintaining an underground, or illegal apparatus; and portraying itself as the champion of numerous popular issues, such as lower taxes, higher wages, shorter working hours, better working conditions, civil rights and civil liberties, and educational and social improvements, all with a wide range of emotional appeal.

To expand its influence in the field of organized labor, the party has established special party commissions to direct its efforts in infiltrating the steel, automobile, and other basic industries. Party leaders are making increased use of propaganda both to expand their influence and to belittle the United States. While

COMMUNIST PROPAGANDA

Propaganda is the Communists' most powerful and effective weapon for influencing, conditioning, and manipulating people.

CHIEF METHODS OF DISSEMINATION IN UNITED STATES

 **NEWSPAPERS AND MAGAZINES**

Newspapers, magazines, and foreign-language newspapers published in U. S.—as well as foreign magazines (printed in English) published in Communist countries—giving current Communist line.

 **BOOKS AND PAMPHLETS**

Domestic and foreign books and pamphlets (printed in English) consisting of Marxist-Leninist classics, eulogies of Red nations, condemnations of U. S., etc.

  **MISCELLANEOUS PRINTED MATTER**

Leaflets, posters, and stickers dealing with current issues.

DEMONSTRATIONS

Public gatherings—such as indoor and outdoor mass meetings, parades, marches, strikes, picket lines, delegations, and public hearings—exploiting social, economic, or political issues.

 **COMMUNICATIONS**

Telegrams, letters, post cards, petitions, resolutions, and statements directed to public officials and non-Communist press voicing protests and demands.

 **ENTERTAINMENT**

Songs, phonograph records, plays, and motion pictures (both domestic and foreign) glorifying Communist-bloc countries and communism and criticizing United States and free enterprise system.

 **RADIO**

Short-wave broadcasts in English beamed at United States from Radio Moscow, Radio Prague, Radio Peking, and other Iron Curtain countries presenting positive picture of economic, scientific, and cultural accomplishments of Red nations.

 **FRONT ORGANIZATIONS**

Formed to appeal to various American propaganda target groups—minorities, youth, women, etc.—to promote cause of communism.

launching new publications and expanding the circulation of existing publications, they are also using radio, television, and personal appearances.

Special emphasis is placed by the party on penetrating the major Negro protest and improvement associations in an effort to exploit all controversial or potentially controversial racial issues. However, one of the bitterest disappointments of the Communists has been their failure to lure any significant number of our Negro citizens into the party.

Sabotage Potential

Because the Communist Party, USA, is a highly disciplined and militant organization dedicated to the spread of world communism and the overthrow of the United States government, the possibility that any Communist in the United States will commit sabotage at any time can never be dismissed. There are, however, a number of reasons the party leadership does not stress sabotage as a tactical weapon at the present time.

Fear of long prison terms for violation of federal laws and the realization that FBI penetration might uncover any plans for sabotage dictate that the party temporarily refrain from using this tactic. Communists have never rejected the use of terror and insurrection, but stress that they must be used when the "time is ripe." At present, the party realizes that it has more to lose by resorting to sabotage prematurely than it could gain by such acts of terror. However, attempts at sabotage will be a major factor in its tactics whenever the Communist Party, USA, believes that an attempt to overthrow the American government might be successful.

Emphasis on Youth

It is among the youth of our nation that the party is concentrating its efforts to expand its influence. In so doing, the party acknowledges a directive of the Moscow Declaration of 1960, which said: "There are new opportunities now to draw the younger generation into the struggle for peace and democracy, and for the great ideals of communism."

A meeting of young Communists and party leaders was held

COMMUNIST FRONT ORGANIZATIONS

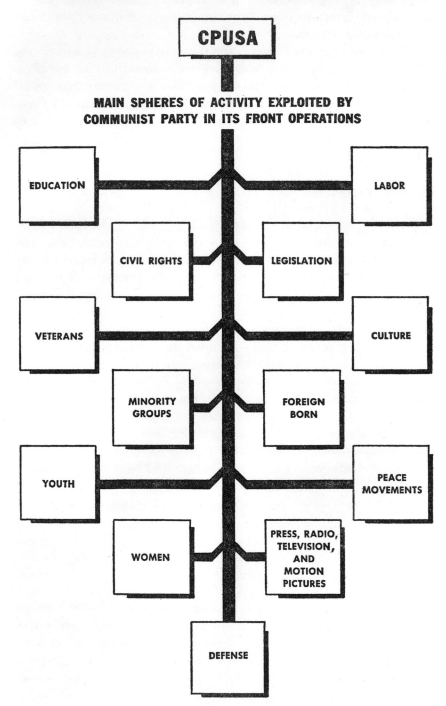

CPUSA

MAIN SPHERES OF ACTIVITY EXPLOITED BY
COMMUNIST PARTY IN ITS FRONT OPERATIONS

EDUCATION

LABOR

CIVIL RIGHTS

LEGISLATION

VETERANS

CULTURE

MINORITY GROUPS

FOREIGN BORN

YOUTH

PEACE MOVEMENTS

WOMEN

PRESS, RADIO, TELEVISION, AND MOTION PICTURES

DEFENSE

at the party's New York City headquarters in May, 1959. At this meeting, plans were formulated to concentrate on colleges and universities in promoting a Marxist orientation among students as the first step in their eventual recruitment into the party. As a part of this campaign among the youth, a Marxist youth periodical, *New Horizons for Youth,* was launched in October, 1960.

To convey Marxism-Leninism to college and university students, party leaders have established a "lecture bureau" and welcome every opportunity to speak before student groups throughout the country. By purporting to present communism in its true light, they avail themselves of the opportunity to take advantage of the natural inquisitiveness of students to learn more about everything including communism.

The corps of Communist lecturers consists solely of speakers who distort the facts and misrepresent communism in order to create a false picture. At the same time, they seize every opportunity to criticize American democracy and American institutions. In this manner, they hope to sow the seeds of discontent in order to create disorder and reap the benefits. A well-organized minority can be effective when its true aims and purposes are concealed.

By taking advantage of the academic freedom in our colleges and universities, Communist lecturers also hope to gain respectability by presenting themselves as representatives of just another political party in the United States. In this manner, they hope not only to obtain recruits but also to gain support for their contention that they are being "persecuted" for their beliefs.

We are proud of the fact that everyone in the United States is guaranteed the right to express his viewpoints. The Communists, like everyone else, are entitled to their beliefs. Under our constitutional guarantees of freedom of speech, all of us, including the Communists, may, within the limitations of the law, freely present our viewpoints. In the market place of public opinion, these viewpoints compete for acceptance. There, in the tradition of our free society, reason must compete with error and truth must compete with falsity.

Knowing this, the Communists do not compete on fair or equal terms in the realm of ideas. They must resort to distortion and misrepresentation. Moreover, they must also, because of the very nature of communism, attempt to impose their views on everyone else. When those beliefs leave no freedom of choice for either their acceptance or their rejection, free men have no alternative but to oppose them firmly. It must be remembered that not a

single country has ever voted the Communists into power in a
free election and that the Communist Party, USA, is part of an
international movement that teaches the necessity for force, violence, and revolution to accomplish its objectives.

A Federal Judge in Detroit made this point in 1954 when sen-
tencing six party leaders who had been convicted for conspiring
to violate the Smith Act. Drawing on his experiences during the
long trial, United States District Judge Frank A. Picard told
them:

> Your admiration for Russia is so great that there isn't any
> doubt in my mind, and there wasn't any doubt in the jury's
> mind, that there is nothing you wouldn't do—lie, cheat,
> or even worse—in order to attain your objectives . . . There
> were times during this trial when I felt that you just de-
> spised capitalists and brass hats because you weren't one of
> them. I have discarded that thought. This morning I'm
> giving you the benefit of saying you believe in your cause
> but whether you do or not is immaterial for that cause has
> so engulfed your thinking, so dominated your every move
> to the extent that five of you took the stand and lied about
> what you believe because you thought the end justified the
> means. . . . You really think you are martyrs. But you're
> not going to jail for your beliefs. You're going to jail
> because you want to force those beliefs on others. . . .

Moscow's Seal of Approval

Elizabeth Gurley Flynn, chairman of the Communist Party,
USA, in a speech to the Twenty-second Congress of the Communist Party of the Soviet Union stated that the members of the
delegation of the Communist Party, USA, were deeply grateful
for the high appraisal and words of approval said at the congress
about the Communist Party, USA, by the first secretary of the
Central Committee of the Communist Party of the Soviet Union,
Nikita S. Khrushchev. She said that they would make every effort
to be worthy of such an appraisal.

Only one conclusion is possible from any objective consideration of past and current activities of the Communist Party, USA.
That conclusion is that the Communist Party of the United States
owes its allegiance completely to the Soviet Union and has,

throughout its history, served directly and willingly as an adjunct of Soviet policy. Since its founding, the Communist Party, USA, has consistently formulated its policies and shifted its tactics according to the wishes of Soviet leaders.

Public Appearances of Soviet-Bloc Personnel

One indication that the leadership of the Communist Party, USA, is following the correct Moscow line by establishing a "lecture bureau" is the parallel increase in the number of public appearances by Soviet-bloc diplomatic personnel. The importance which the Soviets attach to public appearances is evidenced by their solicitation of invitations to speak before groups of all types throughout the country. During 1961, for example, Soviet diplomatic officials made 79 appearances in the United States, speaking before 37 student groups, 18 Russian-American and cultural groups, nine religious groups, nine professional groups, and six smaller, miscellaneous groups. In addition, they made 11 television appearances.

Speakers from the "lecture bureau" of the Communist Party, USA, can take their cues from the public addresses of Soviet personnel in the United States. Regardless of the title assigned or the subject matter to be covered, these diplomatic officials invariably manage to work in the current Communist propaganda line on such issues as peaceful coexistence, diplomatic recognition of Communist China by the United States, Cuba, disarmament, and the alleged "imperialistic" policy of the United States. All of this is accompanied by denials that the Soviet Union interferes in the affairs of other nations.

Intelligence and Espionage

Speeches are important to Soviet-bloc diplomats, but of even greater importance are their intelligence-gathering activities. In common usage the terms "intelligence" and "espionage" mean about the same thing. However, for our purposes, "intelligence" will be used to denote the basic, over-all efforts of one country to obtain information about another country. "Espionage" will denote those intelligence operations involving clandestine methods which violate the laws or regulations of another country.

Whether Soviet-bloc representatives in the United States come by material openly or by clandestine means is, in a certain sense, an academic question. The important fact is that behind Soviet-bloc probing and gathering is one sinister purpose: to weaken our nation and to speed the Communists' efforts to gain control of the world.

Targets of Soviet-bloc intelligence and espionage activities in the United States are all-embracing. Many targets are predictable, such as defense plans, or information about weapons development, deployment of military personnel, strategic military and industrial areas, and scientific and industrial advances. Efforts are also made to penetrate government agencies, to ascertain United States foreign policy, and to gather information about anti-Communist emigre groups in the United States.

"Legal" Intelligence Activities

The vast network of Communist intelligence activities in the United States ranges from the overt collection of publicly available information to the secret operations of a spy whose real identity may not be known even to his contact man. In order to comprehend the nature of these extensive Soviet-bloc intelligence operations, it is necessary to view separately each of the components.

Soviet-bloc intelligence activities in our country may be classified under two broad categories, the so-called "legal" and the illegal. These descriptive terms—legal and illegal—are taken right from the Communists themselves. Communists are taught that both a legal and an illegal apparatus must be maintained wherever possible. This practice extends throughout the Communist party organization, and certain aspects of it carry over into Communist espionage networks.

"Legal" to the Communists means the open organization. It is the term they use to refer to the above-ground, as opposed to the underground, party. The so-called legal intelligence network, then, includes some Communists who are openly active in party affairs and official personnel of Soviet and satellite diplomatic and trade establishments in this country. Diplomatic and other official establishments serve as the headquarters for these networks, and diplomatic communication channels are used to relay instructions and to transmit the information developed.

Our government in the United States, operating under the principle that as much information as possible, consistent with national security, should be made public, has a wealth of material available to interested persons. American industry issues volumes of technical and scientific information on manufacturing techniques and industrial processes. American newspapers and magazines carry articles on such subjects as our atomic energy programs, our armed forces, and scientific developments adaptable to military use.

Official Establishments

The facility with which information can be obtained in this country encouraged the Soviets to place very early emphasis on the establishment of official organizations to exploit the vast opportunities most efficiently and effectively. For example, in 1924, the Soviets formed the Amtorg Trading Corporation in New York City. Since that time, Amtorg has served as a convenient means of collecting information in the United States that would aid the development of the Soviet economy.

It was in 1933, however, with United States diplomatic recognition of the Soviet Union, that the Soviets greatly enlarged the foundation upon which they were to build and develop their broad intelligence networks. Today, diplomatic and other official establishments of the Soviet Union and Soviet-bloc countries in this country are numerous, and their intelligence and espionage agents are confident, aggressive, and highly professional.

The total of Soviet official personnel in this country at the Soviet Embassy, the United Nations, Tass (the Soviet official news agency), and Amtorg Trading Corporation is about 400. It is reported by a former Soviet intelligence officer who defected that approximately 70 to 80 per cent of the Soviet officials in this country have some type of intelligence assignments. This figure, of course, does not take into account the additional personnel recruited from the American populace and controlled by these "legal" spies.

In addition to Soviet representatives, officials of other Soviet-bloc countries are stationed in this country. They number around 300 and almost double the potential of the Soviet intelligence services. During the 1950's, Soviet and satellite intelligence operations were blended into a coordinated network operating under

Principal Targets of Soviet-Bloc Intelligence and Espionage Activities in United States

 1. Scientific research and development, with particular attention to satellites, guided missiles, rockets, radar defense, electronics, aeronautics, and atomic energy.

 2. Defense plans, strength, deployment, and training methods of the armed forces, as well as weapons, equipment, and ordinance.

 3. Strategic areas and industrial sites, such as military, naval, and air installations, dams, harbors, railroad yards, steel mills, industrial plants, etc.

 4. Information concerning and penetration of agencies of the United States government.

 5. Foreign policy, such as U.S. position and proposals, conversations between Allied officials, military pacts between U.S. and other nations, etc.

 6. Anti-Communist political opposition groups—emigres and refugees from Soviet-bloc countries and nationality groups in U.S., such as Poles, Hungarians, Czechs, etc.

the guidance of the Soviet Union. Coordination of Communist-bloc intelligence activities is maintained by the presence of Soviet advisors in the satellite countries and by Soviet personnel in this country.

Intelligence Collection Techniques

Soviet-bloc officials use several techniques to collect material. They regularly attend conventions or exhibitions held throughout the United States by industrial, scientific, professional, educational, and trade groups. They collect printed matter and take photographs at "open house" exhibits held for the public at various American military, naval, and air bases. They often use memberships in various organizations to obtain information. Sometimes, these memberships have been obtained by disguising their identities as Soviet-bloc personnel.

Communist-bloc intelligence agents also attend public lectures on industrial progress, engineering developments, nuclear energy uses, political matters, and weather science. They correspond with industrial concerns which offer material to individuals requesting it. Various chambers of commerce have received requests from Soviet-bloc representatives for information concerning their particular areas. In many instances, useful maps have been collected. The Communist agents have, in some cases, disguised their status in this country in order to obtain information.

Soviet-bloc personnel have gathered material by subscribing to numerous newspapers and magazines of a scientific, military, and general news nature. They are known to have subscribed to newspapers published at or near American military bases. Moreover, two registered agents of the Soviet Union in this country— the Four Continent Book Corporation and Tass—have purchased American scientific and technical publications valued at thousands of dollars, in addition to obtaining many free scientific and industrial publications.

According to one defector from Soviet-bloc intelligence, a Communist agent operating in most other countries would have to spend 90 per cent of his time in clandestine activities in order to ferret out the type of information that is readily available in the United States. He reported that the intelligence agency with which he was formerly associated collects more technical data in the United States than from all the other countries of the world combined. In addition, this defector stated that the Soviet military attache's office in the Russian diplomatic mission to this country finds that it can "legally" obtain about 95 per cent of the material collected for intelligence purposes.

The problem posed by overt intelligence collection activities conducted by aggressor nations in free nations is not susceptible of easy solution. Various government committees have wrestled with the situation for years, but, to date, no practical solution has been found which would effectively deny unclassified material to the Communists without seriously interfering with our own use of it. Attempts, so far, to control unclassified information deemed to be of strategic value to the Communists have raised problems of censorship. Programs to prohibit the publication in our nation of such unclassified material are in fundamental conflict with the traditions of American freedom and our concepts regarding the free exchange of information and ideas. Our abiding faith in freedom of expression is one of the vital distinctions between us and the Communists.

Recruiting and Motivation of Agents

Despite the existence of highly trained professional intelligence agents in the United States, the broad range of Communist targets in technical, scientific, industrial, political, economic, and military fields makes it imperative that these "legal" agents recruit help. The professionals need sources of information and helpers to do "leg work," especially in operations requiring secrecy. Even the wealth of information readily available in the United States does not satiate the Soviets' appetite, and they regularly resort to espionage operations, or covert methods, to obtain information.

Soviet-bloc diplomatic personnel utilize several recruiting techniques to obtain continued cooperation. One obvious technique is the payment of money or something of value for services rendered. Often this approach is so subtle that the potential recruit is involved before he knows it and has performed an intelligence assignment which has compromised him. Some individuals have been partially motivated by the momentary thrill of conspiratorial activities.

Others have been recruited because, for some reason, they had a desire for revenge against the United States. Another technique for recruitment and control is the cold-blooded exploitation of a "hostage" situation. When this technique is employed in the United States, it invariably involves an American who has relatives living behind the Iron Curtain. Soviet-bloc diplomatic personnel also evaluate personal weaknesses in order to use blackmail to obtain cooperation.

At the time Khrushchev was preaching "peaceful coexistence and friendly co-operation," at the United Nations in September, 1959, a Soviet spy in the United States was meeting in Springfield, Massachusetts, with a young American of Ukranian descent whom he was attempting to coerce into giving the Soviet Union information regarding our cryptographic machines. The Soviet spy was Vadim A. Kirilyuk, a Soviet employed at the United Nations in New York City. Kirilyuk attempted to obtain cooperation by holding out the offer of a scholarship and funds. The American was also reminded repeatedly that he still had relatives living in the Ukraine. Kirilyuk's activities were brought to the attention of the United Nations Secretary General and shortly thereafter Kirilyuk returned to the Soviet Union.

The opportunities for Soviet-bloc personnel to recruit additional information sources have increased in recent years. Today, a large number of American students, tourists, and businessmen travel abroad, not only to non-Communist countries, but also to Communist lands. Communist intelligence agents, both in their own countries and abroad, will, in their contacts with Americans, evaluate them as potential sources of information.

Communication Methods

Once Soviet-bloc intelligence agents, operating in this country as legal representatives from their homelands, have established an apparatus to obtain intelligence material, it is obvious that their most important requirement is an adequate communications system for the transmittal of instructions or for the receipt of intelligence material. Whether material is received personally, through the mail, or through a system of hiding material in a prearranged location or "drop" for pickup at a later date, it must then be sent from the Soviet-bloc official establishments to the Communist nations. Normally diplomatic channels are used for this purpose.

It is, therefore, easy to see that the diplomatic channels are crucial factors in passing material and instructions back and forth between the Soviet bloc and this country. What would happen if these channels were suddenly severed by the outbreak of war or the cessation of diplomatic relations for some other reason? In order to obtain information at all times and to insure an uninterrupted flow of communications between intelligence agents in this country and the home countries in the event diplomatic channels are closed, the Soviet-bloc countries have set up illegal intelligence networks.

Illegal Intelligence Activities

These parallel networks are engaged in undercover operations. The illegal intelligence network embraces those Communists in the underground apparatus of the party and those individuals who are undercover spies for the Communist world. The illegal, or clandestine, espionage networks are directed by agents who have no overt connection with their Soviet-bloc principals. Their members are in this country, not under diplomatic or other official status, but illegally. Usually, they have entered this country by assuming false identities and utilizing fraudulent travel and identity documents.

In the past, these illegal agents have settled in the United States and have assumed the life of normal American citizens for the purpose of concealing their fraudulent entries. Some have been known to remain in an inactive status for as long as 10 years. As "sleeper agents" they could be activated following a break in diplomatic relations to serve as a means for transmitting information and material to their home countries. In addition to this important potential, illegal agents operate completely under cover to supplement the espionage activities of the Soviet-bloc legal apparatus.

Although illegal agents from the Soviet Union were dispatched to the United States as early as the 1920's, illegal agent operations have been given even greater emphasis since the early 1950's. One former Soviet intelligence officer has advised that a special directorate was created in 1947 to handle illegal agents. Another former Soviet intelligence officer has stated that in 1952 an order was sent to Soviet intelligence agents in Western countries to prepare an illegal organization which could function without interruption under any conditions. In furtherance of this policy, Soviet illegal agents were sent to the United States.

Espionage and Science

Just as a communications system is the life blood of "legal" intelligence activities, so it is with illegal activities. Espionage is like warfare. Scientific advances favor the offense. Eventually, a defense is discovered to counter new weapons but, in the meantime, the offense has a head start. So it is in the field of espionage. First came secret codes, invisible inks, and long-range radios. While the defense was catching up with these, new advances were being made in photography. Documents can now be microfilmed by a camera concealed in the palm of the hand. Then, a microfilmed page can be reduced in size so that it can be hidden in a period or other punctuation mark in what appears to be an innocent document. Blueprints can, by the same method, be reduced and hidden in the center of a hollowed-out coin or other small object.

The battle against such techniques is a continuing one. With a demonstrated technological proficiency, the Soviet-bloc countries are constantly bringing to bear all the most advanced techniques which can be devised to aid their espionage networks and to thwart detection.

Regardless of the secrecy and care with which Soviet-bloc intelligence and espionage operations proceed, their role is to sap the strength of this nation while vitalizing the Communist machine in its efforts to control the world. Like all Communist operations, they are designed to carry out the mandate of the 1960 statement of the 81 Communist parties—to disrupt and weaken the influence and strength of the United States.

The over-all intensification of subversive and intelligence activities against the United States reveals the underlying treachery and deceit in Khrushchev's pious statements about "peaceful co-existence and friendly co-operation." Communists never entertain any ideas of a permanent reconciliation with non-Communists. This was cogently stated during 1962 by Mikhail Suslov, a secretary of the Central Committee of the Communist Party of the Soviet Union, when he said:

> Peaceful coexistence in the ideological sphere, any reconciliation, even a temporary compromise with the bourgeois ideology both in the internal and external spheres are impossible. This is impossible without betraying the interests of communism. This would mean the ideological disarmament of the communists, the disarmament of the international working class movement.

Chapter 12

Meeting the Communist Challenge

If the history of communism and our experience in dealing with it have taught us anything, it is that we must view all Communist activities on the international, national, and local levels as different aspects of the total and continuous struggle the Communists are waging to bring about our destruction.

We did not create this struggle. It was set in motion in 1917 when the Communists in Russia overthrew and smashed a liberal, democratic government to establish their own brand of dictatorship. It was their intent then—and it has been their goal ever since—to establish a world-wide Communist dictatorship by any and all means. The Communists are waging this total struggle against the non-Communist world with a variety of weapons. They are active in all areas of human endeavor with relentless vigor and do not consider themselves bound by any of the traditional moral or legal restraints.

No rational, informed person can doubt that the Communist world poses a direct and threatening challenge to free men everywhere. It is a challenge which assumes many forms. It is a challenge which, while modern in form, is ancient in substance. It is, in essence, a struggle between freedom and tyranny. Freedom has always had to contend with tryanny. Freedom must be constantly won and rewon. It cannot survive unless those who cherish freedom are prepared to nourish, live by, defend, and develop it.

Unlike communism, freedom cannot be imposed upon anyone. It must always be sought and, if necessary, fought for.

While communism must be achieved and maintained by force, it can never eradicate man's innate desire for freedom—our strongest weapon in the struggle against communism.

Aspects of the Challenge

The basic Communist challenge—the seizure of total power for the imposition of a totalitarian system upon the entire world—is comprised of several specific challenges.

The *political challenge* of communism springs from the Leninist conviction that power, not law, is decisive. As a consequence, Communists are continuously striving to amass more and more political power throughout the world. At present there are Communist parties operating, either legally or illegally, in some 70 free world nations. These Communist parties are, in effect, agents of a foreign power. Their primary objective is not to promote the interests of the countries in which they operate but rather, to support and defend the interests of the world Communist movement. These Communist parties provide the international Communist movement with the unique advantage of controlling its own forces behind the lines of the declared enemy.

Underlying the political challenge and furnishing a solid backing for it is the military capability of the Communist world. While the actual strength of Communist armed forces is a closely guarded secret, the Communist *military challenge* is so well known that there is little need to dwell on it. We are all aware of the Communists' nuclear capabilities, the tremendous thrust of their military rockets, their large submarine fleet, their huge standing armies, and their modern air force. Soviet Premier Khrushchev recently gave the world a grim warning of the Communist military challenge when he announced that Soviet scientists have developed a nuclear bomb with the explosive power of 100,000,000 tons of TNT.

The Communist *scientific challenge* is a direct adjunct of its military challenge and is largely responsible for the threat posed by Communist military power. Whether we like it or not, we are in a race for scientific and technological supremacy, and the long-term security—if not the very existence—of free societies may well depend on the outcome. The Communists are intent on gaining world scientific leadership, realizing fully that pre-eminence in this field can exert a decisive influence upon world leadership in other areas.

The Communist world has devised an educational program which is specifically designed to attain world supremacy in science. This *educational challenge* is one of the most significant aspects of the over-all Communist challenge. The Communist educational program continuously selects the best young minds, finances their schooling, trains them thoroughly for specific scientific careers, and offers powerful incentives to stimulate them to outstanding effort. Under the current emphasis on scientific training, the student's life is oriented toward achievement of one goal—attaining scientific and technological progress—and the results are solid evidence that, for Communist purposes, their educational system is frighteningly effective.

The concentrated effort being made by the Communists to surpass the non-Communist world in industrial production makes their *economic challenge* an increasingly formidable one. The Soviet economy is rising fast, and the USSR is intent on further accelerating its economic development. The program adopted by the Twenty-second Congress of the Communist Party of the Soviet Union projects an increase of 150 per cent in total industrial output within 10 years and a 500 per cent increase during the next 20 years. At the same time, the Communists are waging all-out economic warfare to capture non-Communist markets and are using trade and economic aid to facilitate Communist penetration of the underdeveloped areas of the world.

All of these Communist challenges—the political, the military, the scientific, the educational, and the economic—are held together by the cement of Communist ideology. Marxism-Leninism provides the ideological basis for these specific Communist challenges. This atheistic and materialistic ideology, with its flexible and pragmatic concept of morality, represents a strong challenge to every other system of thought.

These specific challenges of communism are frequently interdependent. But they can also work separately to confront and to confound free men everywhere. Moreover, the cumulative effect of Communist successes in all of the areas where they challenge us has given rise to still another Communist challenge—*the psychological.* Communists have always insisted that the triumph of communism is historically inevitable. Now, based on the formidable power which has been amassed by the Communist empire, the theme of the invincibility of communism has been added to the claim of its inevitability. By hammering at these confident themes, the world Communist movement is attempting to portray communism as the onrushing wave of the future, against which all opposition is futile. This powerful psychological weapon is intended to instill a defeatist attitude in the minds of non-Communists.

"What Is To Be Done?"

These, then, are the basic challenges of communism which must be met and defeated by free men. Lenin's study, *What Is To Be Done?* although published in 1902, is still hailed by Communists everywhere as a classic. This study serves as a guide for Communists throughout the world who are building their revolutionary parties according to the pattern developed by Lenin. Today, confronted with the challenge which communism has hurled at the world, free men are asking themselves, "what is to be done?"

There are many Communist activities, particularly those involving espionage and the underground apparatus, with which the average citizen cannot directly contend. Nor would it be desirable for the average citizen to play a direct role in combating them. To meet effectively the Communist subversive thrusts, it is essential to employ highly professional counterintelligence measures—measures for which the average citizen is neither equipped nor trained. Modern-day counterintelligence, with its emphasis on professional skills and training as well as its reliance on competent scientific aids, is a task for experts.

Role of the Citizen

Nevertheless the citizen in any free society has a vital role in combating communism. Moreover, it is a demanding role. It demands wisdom and understanding of the Communist forces which would destroy us. The citizen must inform himself about the real nature of communism in order to develop a greater understanding of what it is, what it is not, how it operates, what its goals are, and why people are attracted to it. Such factual knowledge of communism will enable the citizen to comprehend the true nature of the Communist conspiracy and thus be alerted to prevent it from making further inroads into our society through internal subversion.

If there is one thing the Communists understand it is power. Communism is an ideology of power. Communism respects only power. Communism is deterred only by power. *But wherever the people are really informed there is also fundamental strength.* In a democratic society, it is the duty of the government to keep the people informed. It is equally the duty of each citizen to insure that he is informed.

It is obvious, of course, that no real defense can be maintained against communism unless our government continues to move positively and firmly to protect our freedoms. The capacity of our government to do this depends upon the alertness and understanding of every citizen. The individual citizen must support effective countermeasures directed by our government against communism in all its forms.

Finally, the citizen must develop and enrich, in a positive fashion, our greatest weapon against communism—individual freedom under law. He must understand and appreciate what freedom really is and must live his individual, family, and community life in the responsible manner which this freedom demands.

A Word of Caution

In dealing with communism, citizens should refrain from making private investigations. Information which comes to an individual's attention regarding communism should be furnished to the FBI, and the checking of the data should be left to trained investigators. Private inquiries may even jeopardize investigations in progress. In cases involving espionage, for example, it is often far more important to identify other members of a spy network, their contacts, sources of information, and methods of communication than to make an immediate arrest.

Moreover, citizens should not circulate rumors about subversive activities or draw conclusions from information which may come to their attention. The information an individual receives may be incomplete or only partially accurate, and, by drawing premature or ill-founded conclusions or circulating rumors, he can often cause grave injustice to innocent people. Vigilante action weakens our free society. It is just as important to protect the innocent as to identify our enemies.

The responsibility for curtailing and containing communism is one for legally constituted authorities acting with the steadfast cooperation of every loyal citizen. This is not the time for inaction nor is it the time for vigilante action. We must unite as a people. We must understand our basic American heritage under law, and we must face the threat of communism with deliberation, quiet courage, and knowledge. These are the qualities from which communism shrinks—these are the qualities against which communism can never succeed.

Reckless charges against individuals and false statements about the nature of communism and the extent of its penetration into various areas of our life serve the cause of communism by creating disunity among Americans. Too often, the label "Communist" is used indiscriminately against those whose views are unpopular or merely differ from those of the majority. Too often, every adverse development is attributed to communism. Misidentification of communism can lead only to disunity and irrational fear. Moreover, it divides us as a nation at the very time we need unity and strength to face the actual and very real threat of communism.

Knowledge Is Vital

In the area of individual and group action by citizens, knowledge of communism is vital. It is essential that action be based on facts. Just as there is danger of apathy due to ignorance of the true nature of communism, so, too, there is danger of defeatism due to over-estimation of the threat of communism.

Freedom and Security

The fundamental problem of protecting our internal security is not a new one. It existed long before the rise of the Communist movement. Since the earliest attempts of man to establish order through government, security has been a fundamental consideration. It is unfortunate that freedom and security are too frequently considered as mutually exclusive. Actually, the hard-won experience of those who have achieved freedom has demonstrated convincingly that the two are closely interdependent. To be free, and to remain free, man must be relatively secure. He must enjoy the stability of order created and maintained by law. Likewise, to be secure—to achieve the stability of order through justice under law—man must have freedom.

Among the laws which are essential to the existence of any government are those which protect it against such crimes as treason, sedition, espionage, and sabotage. Since the rise of international communism, many laws have been adopted to meet the specific threats resulting from the multi-pronged attack being made against us. However, experience has shown that the sheer volume of laws regarding internal security is not necessarily a real measure of their effectiveness. Nowhere is this more evident than in its application to Communist activities.

Indoctrinated in conspiratorial methods, Communists are adept at evading laws designed to restrict their activities. Necessarily, most laws relating to internal security are developed from past experience, rather than from anticipation of future problems. As a result, there may be an unavoidable delay between the time when a specific threat to security is identified and the time when legal steps can be taken to meet it. Communists, on the other hand, are long-range conspirators who plan far into the future. Therefore, as a practical matter, government legislation and regulations, in and of themselves, will not guarantee our security.

Individual Responsibility

We are proud of our constitutional form of government by which the people delegate powers to their government. This system not only limits the powers of the government, but also restricts the areas in which these delegated powers may be applied. These limits on governmental authority are a heritage of freedom which all Americans jealously guard. These limits, necessarily and desirably, place the ultimate burden of responsibility for the security of the nation squarely upon the shoulders of the individual citizen.

In fulfilling his responsibility, the individual citizen must be more than *alert* to the dangers of communism and its conspiratorial operations. He must be vitally *concerned* with the establishment of measures, on all levels of American life, which will remedy or improve those social, psychological, political, and economic factors exploited by Communists to gain support for their cause. In this positive manner, Communist efforts to capitalize on the misfortunes of others will be thwarted.

The importance of the individual citizen in our system is recognized by the leaders of the international Communist movement. Despite Communist propaganda about the so-called ruling circles in the United States, Communist leaders know that the ultimate power in our nation rests in the hands of the people. Therefore, they exploit every opportunity to appeal to the people over the heads of the leaders of our government, realizing that public opinion is a determining factor in our government's actions.

Communists believe that this governmental responsiveness to the will of the people is a weakness that will contribute to our downfall. They see in their own system, marked by its ability to marshal and direct a regimented society toward selected goals without any question, a greater capacity to achieve domestic and international objectives. Since there is no need to consider the will of the people, Communist leaders are able to concentrate on a single objective and move swiftly toward it. There is little doubt that many Communist achievements to date have been made possible by this totalitarian "efficiency." Not to be overlooked, however, is the characteristic ruthless power which disregards the cost in human lives, human values, and human freedoms.

Can Freedom Compete?

In essential terms we must ask: Can we, as an open society based on democratic principles and adherence to individual freedom under law, compete effectively with world communism, a totalitarian society uninhibited by traditional moral scruples and legal restraints and dedicated to world domination?

Competition with a totalitarian system is, indeed, difficult. It is even more difficult to compete with a Communist totalitarian system—a system which, as a matter of both ideological dedication and state policy, operates the most extensive networks of subversion ever known to the world. In this competition, the wide diversity of freely formed opinions and ideas which we Americans hold is too frequently mistaken for a symptom of weakness. Yet, it is the interaction of diverse views, under our system of freedom under law, which is largely responsible for our greatness as a nation.

The ultimate advantage of our free society over the Communist totalitarian state lies in the diverse and imaginative thinking and resourcefulness of the free individual. These attributes can always overcome any temporary advantage which ruthless discipline may produce in the Communist system. On the surface, dictatorships appear to enjoy an advantage over democracies. Yet, history has demonstrated that dictatorships frequently are weaker than they appear, while free nations usually are stronger than they seem to be.

Freedom—Key to the Future

Throughout history, man has been confronted with a never-ending struggle against tyranny. However, history has shown that free societies have invariably proved more resilient, creative, and enduring than those under a totalitarian yoke. The ultimate guarantee against Communist encroachment is a deep and abiding awareness on the part of each citizen that freedom is inherently superior to communism. Communists falsely pose the issue as one between communism and capitalism. In reality, the struggle is one between freedom and tyranny. And, when communism is finally defeated, it will not be a victory of capitalism over communism or of the United States and its allies over the Communist bloc. It will be the victory of freedom over tyranny.

Freedom is the one value which underlies and is an inherent part of all other values. Only under freedom do other values acquire real meaning. Only under freedom can other values grow. Without freedom, all other values lose their lustre; some, in fact, lose all meaning.

What value is there in prolonging human life through medical science if that life must be lived in slavery? What value is there in achieving a high rate of literacy, if the individual is not free to read and write the truth? What value is there in a high rate of voter participation if there is no choice of candidates? What value is there in advanced scientific inquiry, if it is channelled in support of a predetermined political position?

America is not a *status quo*. It is, instead, a dynamic idea. The values and benefits—both spiritual and material—which have flowed from this idea into our lives were not developed by accident. Nor were they developed, as the Communists claim, through economic determinism. They were achieved by the morally conscious effort of self-reliant individuals acting independently or by joining together for a common purpose made possible by common agreement on fundamental principles. The values we revere as Americans have been constantly and deliberately redefined, rewon, developed, and enriched by each succeeding generation learning from the past to chart the course for the future. In this period of crisis, we must revitalize our proven values of the past and merge them with the opportunities of the present. Then we will have more than enough determination and moral strength to meet and defeat the challenge of communism while moving ahead on the basis of our own freely chosen values.

America was founded on freedom. It has grown and prospered, spiritually and materially, under freedom. And, in its deep and abiding faith in the ultimate triumph of freedom, America still holds the key to the future of mankind. With faith in the inherent dignity and worth of the individual, Americans can face the future with vitality and resolute purpose.

Part Six

A Digest of Differences

Basic Contrasts:
Communism versus Freedom

Communism, as we have seen, is a direct assault on individual freedom—the very foundation of our society. The conflict in which we are engaged touches upon every aspect of human endeavor. Even more basic, however, it is a conflict between two diametrically opposed concepts of the meaning of human life itself.

Communism—an atheistic and materialistic philosophy—claims, in effect, that man is only what he eats; that there is only a difference of degree, not an essential difference, between human and other forms of life; that morality is based on expediency; that history is a purely materialistic process in which the economic factor is decisive; and that all life ends at the grave. Under communism, power is decisive, and the individual exists only for, and at the will of, an all-powerful state.

Our way of life is based on the conviction that man does not live by bread alone, but also by spiritual values. We hold that, because man has been endowed by his Creator with a spiritual soul destined for immortality, every human being has inherent dignity and worth.

We are convinced that a Supreme Being guides the destinies of men through a Divine Providence. Because our actions are guided by the traditional Judaeo-Christian moral law, we have intrinsic standards of what is right and what is wrong. Under freedom, law—not power—is decisive, and each individual has certain unalienable rights which can never be abrogated by the state.

The following comparison illustrates, simply and graphically, the essential differences between communism and the freedoms we enjoy in the United States.

Communism   vs.   Freedom

Aims

Communism	Freedom
Communism is dedicated, by ideology and practice, to complete domination of the world. Communism aims to destroy all other social orders and to communize the entire world.	Freedom is dedicated to peace and liberty for human beings to pursue many goals.
Communism advances its cause regardless of any cost to and demand on the individual.	Freedom supports the right of the people of all countries to select their own social orders. Freedom promotes the general welfare, insures justice, and guarantees life, liberty, and the pursuit of happiness for all.

Criticism

Under communism, the individual is pressured to accept whatever the state decrees.	Freedom emphasizes the right of the individual to criticize and to advocate change and reform.
Voicing of dissent is strictly controlled and severely punished.	Voicing of dissent is encouraged, not restricted.
Thought control, as an established state policy, enforces an acceptance of the *status quo*.	The right to exchange ideas and to criticize provides a dynamic process for the constant improvement of society.

Methods of carrying out policy can be criticized, but not the validity of the policy itself.

Any aspect of policy, its correctness or its execution, can be freely questioned.

Conformity to Communist thought and action is achieved by party control.

Conformity is not the aim of freedom, which benefits from the process of open discussion and criticism.

Economy

The economy is totally planned, directed, and controlled by the state.

Our free-enterprise economy is based on competition.

The needs of the state determine production, wages, and prices.

Basically, the law of supply and demand governs production, wages, and prices.

Lack of competition minimizes the incentive to improve the quantity, quality, and diversity of products.

Normally, the demands of the open market force the producer to improve the quantity, quality, and diversity of products.

Forced or slave labor has been an integral part of the economy.

Slave labor does not exist.

While the state concentrates on heavy industry and armaments, the public suffers from a chronic shortage of housing and consumer goods.

Generally, housing and consumer goods are produced in direct response to customer demands and preferences.

Education

The goal of education is to advance the cause of communism.

Education is pointed toward the development of the individual.

The educational system trains youth for subservience, obedience, and conformity to the state.

The educational system helps prepare the student for a career of his own choice and assists him in becoming a well-rounded, responsible, self-reliant, individual.

Art and science serve the interests of the state by extolling life in the Communist world and strengthening the Communist bloc.

Art and science are unfettered, and the individual is free to utilize his artistic or scientific talents toward the unrestricted advancement of culture and science.

Teachers are compelled to conform to the Communist party line.

Teachers enjoy academic freedom.

Elections

Elections do not express the will of the people.

Elections are the voice of the people.

Elections are held only when the government decrees.

Elections are conducted regularly as specified by law.

Only one slate of candidates—that chosen by the "elite" in the Communist party—appears on the ballot.

A choice of candidates is offered the voters.

The outcome of an election is predetermined, since only the Communist party candidates appear on the ballot.

There is no predetermined outcome to an election, for the result rests on the free choice made by the voters.

Employment

The worker is restricted to his work by various governmental regulations, among which are the labor book and the internal passport.

The worker is free to choose his own occupation.

A worker may quit his job only for reasons approved by the state and then only with the permission of his plant manager.

An individual can resign from a job for any reason and at any time he sees fit without penalty or punishment.

Wages, hours, and other matters of vital concern to workers are excluded from the scope of labor-management discussions.

Collective bargaining covers all aspects of labor-management relations, including wages, hours, fringe benefits, working conditions, etc.

Government

The Communist party rules through a totalitarian government with absolute powers.

Freedom provides a constitutional government with power derived from the people.

Communism maintains a dictatorship with no regard for the people.

Freedom makes possible a government of, by, and for the people.

The will of the Communist state is supreme.

Under freedom, the will of the people is supreme.

The individual exists to serve the state.

The government exists to serve the individual.

Communism means a government of men and not of laws.

Freedom means a government of laws and not of men.

Minority rule prevails.

Majority rule prevails.

The ruling group, with a monopoly of power, is not accountable to the people.

The people have the dominant voice in their government and officials are responsible to them.

Public opinion is not a determining factor in the formulation of national policy.

Public opinion is a decisive factor in the establishment of national policy.

Communism recognizes no popular right to alter or amend the existing government so as to reflect the desires of the people.

Freedom does recognize the popular right to alter or amend the existing government.

There is merely a theoretical separation of executive, legislative and judicial powers in a Communist state.

Freedom provides for an effective separation of powers as a means of checks and balances.

The Communist party determines the policies and writes the laws of the country.

Only elected officials responsible to the people determine the nation's policies and write its laws.

Removal of policy-making government officials arises primarily from factionalism or death.

Government policy-making officials are periodically removed through the process of free elections.

Political dissidents are ousted from the government and the Communist party and thereafter deliberately disgraced, ostracized, and, in some cases, executed.

Political opponents enjoy full freedom to criticize and to appeal their cause to the people with no fear of repression or punishment.

Fear, terror, and force are used as weapons to win and to hold total power.

The consent of the majority is required for the exercise of constitutionally limited power.

Human Rights

There is a total disregard for the inherent dignity of the individual.

There is a deep and abiding respect for the inherent dignity and the worth of the individual.

The state asserts and retains full and complete power over the individual.

The state recognizes and respects certain God-given unalienable rights of the individual.

A Communist constitution is nothing more than propaganda window dressing and guarantees only continued Communist domination.

The Constitution is meaningful and is designed to guarantee human dignity and freedom.

There is a complete denial of individual freedom.

All laws are designed to provide the maximum of individual freedom consistent with the rights of others.

Freedom of speech, the press, and assembly are permitted only to the extent that they support official policy.

Freedom of speech, the press, and assembly are protected not only in constitutional guarantees but in practice.

Media of mass communication such as newspapers, magazines, radio, and television are strictly controlled by the government.

Media of mass communication are free to praise or criticize without fear of government control.

Rights and privileges are doled out as rewards for service to the state.

The rights of all are guaranteed by law.

Law

Law is an instrument of force and is inseparable from political control.

Law, to be just and effective, must be separate from and independent of political control.

The function of law is to subordinate man to the state.

The function of law is to guarantee individual liberty while protecting the rights of all other individuals in society.

Proof of innocence is the responsibility of the accused.

Innocence is presumed until guilt is proved.

Any citizen can be detained at the discretion of the state if he is considered "socially dangerous."

No person can be deprived of life or liberty without due process of law.

Citizens can be and are easily denied an open trial.

Every citizen is entitled to a speedy, public trial by an impartial jury.

Since the courts are instruments of the ruling Communist party, the proceedings of trials are followed closely by the party and subject to its influence.

A secret police exists and operates to enforce the dictates of the state.

The outcome of trials is never predetermined, for every defendant is guaranteed a fair public trial by a jury of his peers.

A secret police is nonexistent, and the individual is protected against arbitrary police action by due process of law.

Political Parties

The Communist party does not and will not share power with other political parties.

Communist party membership is restricted to a highly select, comparatively small group.

The existence of a multiparty system provides a restraint on power.

Membership in any political party is broad and unrestricted.

Property

Private property rights are strictly limited.

The individual can own only personal property, household goods, and real estate on which he can make no income.

The right to acquire, enjoy, and hold private property is protected.

People have the right to purchase, rent, and sell real and personal property.

Religion and Morality

Outlook on life is based on materialism.

Outlook on life is based on spiritual concepts and traditions.

Communism strives to destroy religion in order to create the dehumanized "Communist man."

Religious freedom is guaranteed but every individual is free to follow his own conscience regarding belief or nonbelief.

Religious groups are restricted in their activities by the state, which claims to provide for all the needs of man.

Religious groups are free to minister not only to the spiritual but also to many other needs of man.

Religious training of youth is controlled to reduce and eventually eliminate religious influence.

Freedom recognizes and respects religious training as a means of strengthening the moral and spiritual fiber of the people.

Communist morality justifies any thought or action which advances the ends of communism.

Morality is based on the traditional principles governing human conduct.

Trade Unions

Trade unions are adjuncts of the state.

Trade unions are independent and self-governing organizations, free of control or influence by the government or by management.

The function of unions is to increase production, to insure labor discipline, and to administer the social insurance system.

The function of unions is to improve the wages, hours, and working conditions of their members.

The state establishes wages, hours, and working conditions.

Trade unions have the right to negotiate with management on wages, hours, and working conditions.

Travel

Internal passports are required for identification and travel, and changes of address must be reported to the police.	The individual may change his address at will.
Citizens are isolated from the outside world by fortified borders.	Travel to other countries is widespread and commonplace.
Spontaneous contacts with foreigners within the country are discouraged.	Contact with foreign visitors is unrestricted.

Index